Flourish

Redefine success and
create more time, energy,
impact and happiness

BIANCA BEST

RETHINK PRESS

First published in Great Britain in 2019 by Rethink Press
(www.rethinkpress.com)

Cover image © Jo Thorpe Photography

Praise

'This is a transformational guide for ambitious women buffeted by the whirlwind of modern life. *Flourish* offers a practical antidote to the ephemeral pursuit of "balance", encouraging women to redefine success on their terms and stop cycles of burnout once and for all. Bianca's six-step programme teaches simple, effective routes to maximise impact and joy. A bible for alpha females!'

Baroness Karren Brady CBE
Vice Chairman of West Ham United FC, TV Presenter and author of *Strong Woman: The Truth About Getting to the Top*

'*Flourish* is a must for anyone figuring out how to achieve exceptionally big goals yet avoid burnout. Peppered with beautiful quotes and practical tips, Bianca takes us on a fun and frank rollercoaster ride of her personal journey along the way.'

Lindsay Pattison
Chief Client Officer, WPP

'*Flourish* provides great solutions to endlessly chasing balance, by teaching practical ways for women to step into a realm of happy, impactful productivity.'

Nicola Mendelsohn CBE
VP Facebook EMEA

'Bianca has captured perfectly the traps we unconsciously build for ourselves in pursuit of success. An honest account of the knock-on effects of burnout, and a practical framework to change the way we define and design success for ourselves.'

Rekha Mehr MBE
Founder and CEO, Moonrekha Innovations

'For amazing women pursuing success in all aspects of their lives, Bianca proffers a thoughtful guidepost to seize life in balance. Based upon real-life experiences, and studied and practical methods, this book is important to women and all of us on our journeys today. *Flourish* also illustrates that fun, joy and happiness can be achieved all along the way. Bianca is living proof of that!'

Barry Frey
President and CEO, DPAA

'An entrepreneur, true leader in the media industry and mother of four who is bursting with positive energy and passion in everything she does. When I met Bianca at AdWeek I had one question: how does she do it? I'm very happy that she has shared her practical programme featuring stories from both her business and private life, and pays so much attention to energy and how we can increase it. A must-read for all alpha females – and not only!'

Barbara Soltysinska
Co-founder and CEO indaHash

'*Flourish* is such a timely book, based on one extraordinary woman's personal journey to find a practical balance between professional and personal responsibilities.

This inspirational book is an indispensable guide for any woman facing increasing demands on her time and attention.'

Norm Johnston
Global CEO, Unruly

'Bianca's personal story is an adventure and a journey, which she has turned into practical life lessons for growth and happiness. It's great to hear how her own experiences have enriched her life and those of others too.'

Sue Unerman
Chief Transformation Officer, MediaCom, and author of *The Glass Wall: Success Strategies for Women at Work and Businesses that Mean Business*

'In *Flourish,* Bianca organises so brilliantly all the tools and steps for living a meaningful and balanced life, both at work and at home. I highly recommend this wonder-book to anyone wanting thrive, stay grounded and live their best life.'

Kieve Ducharme
VP Growth, MediaMonks

'There's only so long the cyclical rhythms of burnout can last before we need to reassess our life's purpose. Bianca's Energy-SCAPE™ model is a fantastic framework to shift from the negative boom and bust cycles to reach a place of sustained productivity with natural energy flow, lasting joy and happiness. Bianca is living proof, and a true inspiration, of how to consciously transform your life to sparkle from the inside out.'

Omi Ducat
Tech Entrepreneur and Business Coach

'Women have spent years trying to fit in and succeed in male-constructed work ecosystems. It's killing us and we're not succeeding as well as we might. It's time for us to change our mindset. How women *want* to work in the future is how millennials *will* work in the future. Women can and should be the trailblazers. This book gives a fresh and pragmatic perspective on how we can do that.'

Tracy de Groose
Chair Newsworks, CRUK trustee, Chair Beached Ltd

'I laughed out loud and I cried! I also read it in pretty much one sitting. It's engaging. Bianca writes like one of your best mates chatting with you over a glass of wine/cuppa but, that said, an intelligent and articulate one with a fine line in self-awareness and self-deprecation. A beautiful guide to living more and stressing less: unflinching, practical and realistic. An essential read for any woman juggling a career with the school run. I loved it!'

Lizzie Burton
Global Agency Leader, Google

'Women with professional ambition and a home life are constantly facing the fear of failing at work and at home. This book isn't about the theory of succeeding in both; it's written by someone who has made it happen for themselves, and this book will make it a reality for you. There's never been a more important time for women to succeed in business and this work will provide the tools you need to thrive.'

Daren Rubins
CEO, Conker

'This book will change your life. Fact! As well as being exceptionally well written, it will make you cry, laugh and provoke thoughts that will lead to permanent change. This book needs to remain on your desk, by your bed or in your briefcase. Allow yourself the opportunity to imprint life-lasting lessons that will impact your daily life more positively than you could ever imagine.'

Simon Ward
Team GB Athlete and High-Performance Coach

'Looking after our "whole" self enables greater success in all aspects of life. *Flourish* is both inspirational and practical – not to be missed!'

Jacqueline O'Sullivan
Global Agency Senior Director, Verizon Media

'Too many women are working hard, playing hard, and sadly losing respect for ourselves and our natural rhythms along the way. This is a poignant how-to guide, essential for modern-day thriving, which embraces the lot – body, mind and soul.'

Nicolle Begovic
Equestrian Athlete, Dressage Rider,
Mother and Footballer's Wife

'Bianca has been a continued source of inspiration throughout our ten years of working together. She is living proof that women can aspire to have it all – and succeed. Bianca successfully juggles a high-powered job, four children and a busy social life whilst making it look easy! Alongside this, she has always been a trusted mentor and friend. Bianca always offers sound and practical advice, and so I am delighted that others with be able to benefit from this by reading her book!'

Shirley Smith
Global Director, Flashtalking

'As a Speaker Coach, I take great pleasure in helping inspirational leaders connect deeply with their audiences. Bianca's mission, work ethic, values and passion all stood out, and I instantly knew she would make significant impact across her industry. Now, seeing Bianca articulate in *Flourish* all she has learnt, believes and is empowering other passionate women with, I believe that her message will continue to reach and impact the lives of millions. It's a pleasure to be a part of that journey.'

Billal Jamil
CEO, Public Speaking Academy

'In *Flourish* Bianca offers us a new way through, a fresh perspective based on her own very personal journey. She shows us all how we, too, can find fulfilment. I feel her voice, her authenticity, her energy pulsating through every page.'

Charlotte Dahl
Director, Woodreed Creative Communications

For my children, Ashley, Scarlett, Sebastian and Beau. You inspire me every day with your sweet kindness, fresh perspectives and innate joy. Thank you for blessing my life so perfectly.

He has achieved success who has lived well, laughed often, and loved much;

Who has enjoyed the trust of pure women, the respect of intelligent men and the love of little children;

Who has filled his niche and accomplished his task;

Who has never lacked appreciation of Earth's beauty or failed to express it;

Who has left the world better than he found it,

Whether an improved poppy, a perfect poem, or a rescued soul;

Who has always looked for the best in others and given them the best he had;

Whose life was an inspiration;

Whose memory a benediction.

– Bessie Anderson Stanley

Contents

INTRODUCTION

SUCCESS ON WHOSE TERMS?

Today, we're experiencing a new, unprecedented era of female empowerment and corporate ascendancy, but this ride isn't proving easy. Not only are we fighting the political battles for pay, status, equality and flexible working, but privately we're overwhelmed, exhausted and compromising our values in pursuit of 'having it all'. 'Me time' has become mythical. More women than ever collapse into sleep at the end of each day wishing they could momentarily hop off their treadmill. A growing number of women are choosing career over family, believing either/or is the only way. 'Time to breathe' is a commonly accepted life quest for most modern women. Our children are being raised by grandparents or strangers. We deprioritise ourselves without realising how much we are in fact harming ourselves.

Amazing women aren't burning brightly; they're burning out – and burning out young. Women are working hard, playing hard, and sadly losing respect for themselves and their natural rhythms. In all of this drive to succeed and achieve we're also losing our sense of belonging and community.

Do you find your daily routine a battle, a bit of a juggling act? I see vibrant, passionate, talented women enjoying career success, but at the expense of their family time and health. I see other equally vibrant, passionate, talented women too afraid to leave their children, to pursue their dreams and work in careers true to their purpose. I see others so ravaged with work or domestic demands they have little time for sleep, let alone energy for play. Do you see yourself reflected in any or all of these women – perhaps in different aspects of them at different stages in your life? Would you love to unlock the secret to steering a course through your hectic life with serenity and grace – without dropping any of the balls?

I've always been obsessed by progress – most successful women are. There's the joy and flurry of pursuit, energy, effort and gain. We're high achievers and get kicks out of our results. Progress is possible, tangible, exciting. All is great until work gets serious and our personal responsibilities increase. Suddenly, the dream feels tough. There's progress, but at what cost? Productivity now feels like a struggle, as there are just too many areas to manage simultaneously. We keep on smiling on the outside, but inside we're cracking. How the heck can we succeed with so much on our plates?

And what exactly is it that we're seeking? What is success today and why does it feel so elusive? Why does attaining success feel like such a burden for so many? I've spent my lifetime chasing a version of success that's led me to ponder over and over again, 'Why does this feel so hard?' But no more.

As a mother of four, a techpreneur, an industry leader, author, networker, insuppressibly alpha female, nutritionist, runner, wife, friend, and, and, and... there's a sheeny exterior that yells, 'I've got it all.' Yet the truth is far from that. I've been on a long, arduous journey – this gig has been *hard*. I've oscillated from exhilarating entrepreneurial business wins to soul-destroying corporate overwhelm, from domestic bliss to unrelenting personal chaos. I've been purposeful, then I've flailed helplessly. At every step it's taken bucket loads of energy, resilience and effort to keep going. I've given myself relentless mind-over-matter pep talks, and focused onwards and upwards. I've worked so damn hard I've pushed my body and mind to their limits. Many times I've cracked in the wake of frenzied productivity and become useless. I've lost weeks of my life, bedridden with immune collapse. I've lost time, comatose with exhaustion. I've even lost my hair.

Finally, four years ago, I broke the cycle. I discovered a way to achieve success *and* flourish. I stepped into a vibrant, joyful and fun way of giving my all without hurting myself. I discovered utopia: a life that blends work, family, passions, friends, health, fitness and spirituality into a harmonious whole. I found my Zen and, miraculously, everything stopped being a struggle. I banished my burnouts.

What did I do? I looked for patterns in my four decades of establishing myself in the world, from childhood to now, in my early forties. I examined the extrinsic factors that had shaped my beliefs and created the personal models of success I had been chasing. I delved deep inwardly, to explore my motivators, my values and my behaviours. I acknowledged my strengths and weaknesses. I looked at my habits and my decisions. I dissected it all, the good and the awful. What emerged was a plan – a way of consciously seizing control so I could get back onto my rightful path. I course-corrected myself into a realm where I flourish. I now have more time, energy, impact and happiness than I ever dreamed of. The whirlwind has stopped buffeting me because I stopped the whirlwind.

I want to show you how to keep progressing (at your pace, in your way) but without compromise, how to maintain performance in all areas of your life simultaneously without breaking yourself, how to be joyful again and how to define what success looks like for you. I want you to bloom.

The following chapters will take you through the model I applied to myself in six logical steps. My Energy-SCAPE™ programme can transform your life into one of harmonious balance, too. Rediscover your best self, clarify where you're headed and why, and enjoy maximum impact with ease while being fully in the moment. This book will help you to identify your personal energy flow and equip you with the tools to thrive, not merely survive. It's time to step out of the mayhem.

The acronym you'll learn to love is:

E – Energy
S – Self-Awareness
C – Cleanse
A – Action
P – Play
E – Enrich

I'm excited about sharing this programme with you because I and thousands of other burnt-out women know it works. It has enabled me to design management plans to prevent chaos and breakdowns – not just for myself, but for the many women I teach, coach and mentor. The method has yielded success time and time again. It has led to spiritual presence and inner contentment, and deepened the capacity to savour work, family, and every precious moment that matters. It's helped talented, passionate women rediscover their vibrancy. I now offer you this gift.

As Global Managing Director of an emerging technology division for the world's largest media agency I have significant work responsibilities with ambitious results to deliver. I have a team to run, industry ambassadorship to uphold and steep financial targets. I cannot bring anything less than my A game to every day. In my role I orbit a fast-paced universe where the people I work with are inspiring, fast-thinking, fast-moving leaders continuously creating positive change and impact.

At home I have four little (two not so little!) souls, a husband, a father and an exuberant puppy. My household is bustling and fluid with waves of chaotic energy fusing gently into calm serenity and back again. Home pulses with the dynamics of different personalities, wants and needs. As much as it's a sanctuary for my soul, it needs managing, of course.

Within me I have passions and desires for fitness, wellbeing, creative pursuits and helping others through my business. I also love a vibrant social life, deep familial connections and spiritual space.

There are multiple facets to my world, as inevitably in yours too.

We can learn so much from the probing questions others ask of us. What do people ask you for advice on the most? Why do people turn to you as the expert they need? Ask yourself when people come to you. It's revelatory and, top tip for you here, a key to your natural strengths and purpose in this world. In my case, almost daily someone will ask me, "How do you do it?" People are genuinely intrigued by how I keep twirling amidst the myriad elements of my world. Not just fascinated by the practicalities of how I keep so many balls juggling at once but the macro lens of how I keep smiling and sparkling my way through the unending to-do lists and still find time to run, eat well and snuggle with the children each night. So, this book is my 'here's how'. This is how I find time, remain energised and embrace every day with sincere gratitude and joy in my soul. I'm no doctor, scientist nor neurological expert, but I have found a way of seizing life that makes each day a gift and if I can inspire just one reader to make a positive change then my soul twinkles a little brighter.

In these pages I share the methods that work for me and invite you to adopt them too. Right here, right now can represent the moment in time when you stepped vibrantly into your best self. Let's go.

STEPPING OUT OF THE WHIRLWIND

'I wish I could go back and tell myself that not only is there no trade-off between living a well-rounded life and high performance, performance is actually improved when our lives include time for renewal, wisdom, wonder, and giving. That would have saved me a lot of unnecessary stress, burnout, and exhaustion.'
– Arianna Huffington

My tale of energy undulations

As a young girl I was always pursuing goals with vigour. When I started collecting (snail shells, Enid Blyton books or ladybirds – don't worry, I did put them back in the garden each evening!) I was on an uninterruptable mission and it *would* be fulfilled, come hell or high water. Moving into my teens I discovered the joy of literature, devouring every published title of my author *du jour*, often obsessively reading till dawn, never mind school and tiredness. At fourteen I decided it would be a useful life skill to touch type so I got a clackety old typewriter and a hardback tutorial book, and after school I'd race up to my bedroom to teach myself to type. In later years I broke a record for the fastest touch typist on a recruitment agency's roster.

When at seventeen I decided to sculpt the body I wanted, I improved my diet, increased my exercise and quickly achieved my target shape. In every aspect of life, once I set myself a personal goal and layered it with deep emotional attachment I always achieved it. My mantra was, 'Failure is not an option'. (Ironically, I later discovered what a gift failure is. When framed positively failure builds emotional resilience and shows you how to course-correct behaviour to reach your goals. Failure is *always* an option today.)

My home life was one of independent exploration. My parents divorced when I was six. I saw this as a blessing, since my mother quickly remarried and suddenly I had two fathers, double the birthday presents, two beautiful homes to enjoy and extra holidays. By the time I was sixteen I had a stepmother, too, as well as two half-brothers, and two stepbrothers in addition to my sister. Life was full of a variety of influences at home, and in

my student life too I was relishing a hu
social circle at the local sixth-form col

I had two part-time jobs, and I con
my passions in spare moments, learnung
thing from esoteric healing arts to graphology to Cindy
Crawford's stomach crunches. I loved my rich, stimulating life.

Adventuring into adulthood

I left home at eighteen, bravely moving alone to
Clapham, to pursue a writing career with a burgeoning Soho publishing company. I felt free, happy and
my eyes were opened to people, places, corporate life,
money and all that grown-up stuff. I soon met my husband at work and there my adult life was set.

Working in media was exhilarating, and I relished
every day. Despite having an entry-level full-time role,
I continued to pursue my ambitions by doing additional freelance copywriting every evening. I would be
on the tube with my notepad, scribbling promotional
copy for ludicrously generous fees (my clients had no
idea I was a novice writer) and feeling invigorated by
the challenge. I was earning more money than most in
their mid-twenties and I was only nineteen. Best of all,
none of it felt like work.

I began studying for a media degree in central London,
while still enjoying freelance writing and temping for

my old publishing companies. My boyfriend and I by then were in a luxury Fulham flat. The good times were rolling and still none of the effort I put in felt like a challenge. I adored staying up late alone on our Thames-view balcony writing papers on modernity, Nietzsche, the Enlightenment and advertising. I was invigorated by what I was learning. Similarly, I loved leaving lectures to head to the office at 4pm each day, to be back in my publishing bubble, mixing with older, career-entrenched colleagues. What fun we had in the Soho pubs after work, night after night…

After graduation I was instinctively drawn towards the advertising industry, landing a series of roles in client management in top London agencies. Now I was in my twenties, my career was underway, the days long, and the nights and the extended lunches/dinners hard. I recall very little self-care during my media heydays. Breakfasts didn't exist, it was caffeine only until lunch-time, and the lunches themselves tended to be liquid. I had gym membership, but my visits were either the guilty 6am Monday morning 'I will go three times this week' efforts, or the post-work, tipsy-on-wine workout. (Even as I write this, I'm shaking my head at these Crimes Against the Self!)

Life was busy but would that stop me pursuing outside interests? I was ensconced in the ad industry but still piqued by journalism. I loved writing and evolved my passion for communication into wanting to present. Enter my radio journalism stint. I was an official hospital radio DJ, and one evening a week after work

I'd spend an hour driving down to Epsom, in Surrey, to host the late-night programme. These efforts never yielded the big TV break I hoped for, but I'd mastered another life skill and had great fun along the way!

A 365-day sojourn

In 1999 my grandfather died. He was the first close relative I'd lost and I went into deep mourning, which prompted my first spiritual quest as I sought to understand the meaning of life. As a result, my boyfriend and I decided to step out of the rat race and spend a year travelling the world.

A full 365 days to the last minute before our round-the-world tickets expired, we completed our exploration of North America, Australasia and South East Asia, from rainforests to tropical beaches, from monkey caves to endless lily ponds, from elephant riding to night diving, from Buddhism to Hinduism, from clambering over Angkor Wat in Cambodia to millennium celebrations in Sydney Harbour.

The thing with me, as all of you high-achieving, non-stop, progressive women will also relate to, is that soon after starting on the trip I realised I couldn't handle a 'year off'. I didn't want to pause my life for a year. I had major FOMO (fear of missing out). I was afraid of foregoing career progression and life impact, afraid I was distancing myself from potential success and wasting precious time. I was happy to travel and explore – and grateful for the privilege, don't get me wrong – but only if I could be developing personally and moving towards my perception of success at the same time. So I used the year to write and learn. I wrote business plans and designed my future. I studied classic literature, local culture and read about psychology, neuroplasticity and spirituality. Physically, I ran miles every day along spectacular coastal paths or through rainforests, as therapy for the insurmountable guilt I felt for deviating onto what I saw as a road less travelled for the 'successful ones'.

Motherhood bliss

It was home to London in 2000, into an international ad agency for me, and at last a marriage proposal from my long-term partner, Lloyd. Fast-forward four years and it's 2004. I'm now Mrs Best, we live out in Surrey in a pristine semi-detached four-bedroom house and have two perfect children, Ashley and Scarlett. I'm combining motherhood with a home-based career penning copy for global brands, from Honda to Mars. I have a treadmill in the garage, a juicer in the kitchen and live a stone's throw away from Caffè Nero, where I get my daily energy fix on the playgroup run. I have a bustling group of friends, I'm exalting in motherhood, I adore the creativity in my work, I'm close to my family again and once more life feels back on track.

The entrepreneurial phase

It was 14 May 2004, my ten-year 'togetherness anniversary' with my husband, I was breastfeeding four-week old Scarlett, caring for eighteen-month-old Ashley and feeling somewhat housebound as I pondered what I could give my husband that didn't entail a Big Shopping Expedition. I decided to create a gift at home, and in that moment the winds of fate blew open a thrilling new chapter.

I wrote a poem entitled 'A Decade to Remember' and dug out favourite photos from the past ten years – brilliant shots of us, from parties and holidays, to travelling, his proposal, and our tender newborn hospital moments. I resourcefully commandeered a sleek oak box frame from a redundant print and arranged my ode and the photos artfully. Voila, a truly bespoke, heartfelt gift.

In the next few weeks friends who visited asked where I'd bought the gift and could they order one for their impending special occasion. I started to wonder if my spontaneous, time-saving concept was in fact a marketable commodity. I conducted some research and rapidly realised that if you wanted something personalised in the UK in 2004 you'd be lucky if you found a mug with your mother's name on a tacky carousel in Clintons, and that little in the way of genuine personalisation existed anywhere. I started to get tingles of excitement.

Consumer confidence in online shopping was growing, and technology was rapidly enabling faster download times and easier access to web developers, not to mention an exploding plethora of retailers shifting into e-commerce and looking to expand their ranges. I recognised that if I could build a platform connecting customers, retailers and manufacturers in a seamless, frictionless environment I would be on to something. And so The Bespoke Gift Company and my journey as an entrepreneur began. Why not add a little sizzle to life with a newborn and a toddler, eh?

One year later and I was on fire, exuberantly running my now definitely-not-cottage industry from home as it grew into a mini personalised gift empire. I'd set up a production unit and customer services department in my home; signed up every online gift retailer from WH Smith to Tesco, Asda, Prezzybox and more; had concessions in Debenhams; and was running profitably, increasing sales month on month at a hugely exhilarating rate. It was a pacey, exciting and pretty addictive time!

My children were my unwavering priority though, so there was zero childcare during this start-up phase. I was the queen of multi-tasking, servicing orders and my retail accounts during playgroup, nap times or once they were asleep for the night. I didn't sleep much myself as a consequence and my days were filled with a high-cortisol, adrenaline buzz, entertaining the children, motivating my staff, managing my customers.

I was a driving force progressing everything with phenomenal momentum.

In the context of the business, I felt myself grow stronger every day. If I got a rejection it wouldn't thwart me (remember my point around failure as a growth opportunity). When I rocked up to prospective printers with my double buggy to ask them to take my business and they laughed me out of the door or gave me untenable cost models, I decided to invest in the kit myself and manufacture from home. When I couldn't get an agency to take on my web development needs as I was perceived as 'small fry', I assembled my own team of Eastern European developers. When WH Smith wouldn't take my call I badgered them relentlessly, until I was there in the UK head office, signing on the dotted line. I was learning I could achieve *anything* I put my mind to with the right focus, attention, resilience and determination.

Enter the medics

I'd had eczema flare-ups since I was a little girl, but I now moved into a more chronic state of skin inflammation. I developed dermatographism, an uncomfortable condition where your histamine levels reach such a high level that any pressure on the skin forms a gigantic, swollen red welt. So I could, say, scratch the initial 'B' into my arm and within a couple of minutes a raised 'B' would be there, looking like an irritated scar. Pat it and prick it and mark it with B...

The doctors explained to me that I was almost permanently in an acute allergic state and suggested I take antihistamines for the rest of my life. Being naturopathically inclined, I brushed this advice off. I decided to self-medicate and cut down on the high- inflammation foods that had triggered my eczema outbreaks as a child. However, despite my diet modifications, the condition worsened throughout the next decade.

At the same time, my endless energy was running out. Little colds became full-on flu epidemics. In the swim of daily life, I would mainline coffee, vitamin C tablets and homemade green ginger juice (if utterly desperate, Lemsip) and carry on being Mummy, CEO, cleaner, chef, shopper and so on, until – wham, bam! – I was totally and utterly floored. I would not be able to get out of bed. I literally could not stand up because the pain in my head and sinuses was so severe. The flu would degenerate into conjunctivitis, tonsillitis, everyitis… My parents and sister would come to help with the children, my husband would have to take time off work and I would sleep round the clock until I felt ready to get back on the treadmill again, immediately revving back up to 100mph. I never once stepped back to consider why I was in this repetitive cycle of total breakdown.

And so I continued. I didn't know how to do anything other than give my all to my work, to my children, and – so I believed at the time – to myself, with intense gym workouts, staying up even later than my work demanded to journal, and making time to see friends and have 'booze benders' at the weekends. I was once again in a high-functioning world, but with a new level of commitments and an older, slightly more beaten, body.

By the time my firstborn started school, I had a production department in the garage with a local team of workers from my village. I had customer service support in the playroom and the printer in the nursery. I ran the business from the lounge, with staff coming in and out, kicking potties and toys out of the way as the business bloomed. It was a happy, invigorating time and I had wonderful, talented and dedicated people working with me.

Despite more hands the pace didn't slow one jot. Conversely, the pressure increased. I now had people dependent on me for their salaries and personal welfare, plus an ever-increasing volume of customers with rightful expectations of service excellence. Still I kept on going, expanding the business, running the home and caring for the children. Oh, the relief of my mother taking a child or doing a school run for me – the gift of being able to focus single-mindedly on the business for a moment during daylight hours.

Stress busting

Then one day, I cracked. I was very skinny, my hair had thinned dramatically, and I was still riddled with dermatographism and insomnia. I had another 'Binky

Burnout' (as my husband called these episodes) but this time just couldn't seem to regain my mojo. I was referred to immunologists and advised I was having total immune collapse brought on by stress. 'Stress? I'm not stressed! I'm living my dream. I have a wonderful home, family, friends, a scaling business. I'm fit, I juice, I'm in the peak of health… surely?!' Dealing only in the empirical, the doctors instructed me to ease up on my superhuman pace and see if I could identify any areas in my life that were potentially causing me stress.

Well, I was quite perplexed (or stubbornly ignorant). I believed I was thriving, though I knew I felt slightly detached most of the time. Racing so fast through each day I was rarely fully present. I knew sometimes my energy was so high and my brain so speedy that I was breathless, talking as quickly as my thoughts were forming. Friends would jokingly ask me to slow down, as I must have given off an unnatural 'busyness'. I often didn't have time to eat. I often didn't have enough sleep. I was so motivated by honouring my commitments. Deep down I suspected that doing a five-mile race on a Saturday morning might be destructive rather than beneficial, but I did it anyway.

Only when I saw Scarlett mimicking me at playgroup, sitting up at the organiser's desk with a plastic pink mobile phone locked under her neck, head tilted to the side while she typed on the keyboard, did I start to think that maybe this pace was perhaps not only hurting me but others too. It slowly started to sink in that maybe I did need to reflect on what stressors I could remove from my life.

So I packed us up. All four of us. Disregarding school, business and career obligations, we went off to Singapore to stay with one of my dearest friends for a week, followed by another two weeks on a Thai island. I slept and slept and slept. The first three days in Singapore I barely left the guest bedroom. I disconnected myself from all responsibility and liberated my mind for the first time in years. I felt I could breathe again.

I did a lot of thinking over that holiday. I looked at the richness of my life, the abundance, the *apparent* success and tentatively came to acknowledge my Compromise of Self. I *was* having it all, life *was* indeed abundant, I *was* indeed achieving – but only in certain areas. I was by no means thriving; I was in fact breaking myself.

Stepping out of my whirlwind and evaluating the pain points in my fast-paced life was the first of many subsequent transformational moments in my journey. It was revelatory: I had to look inside as well as out.

I came to a grumbling acceptance that I couldn't continue without changing how I was leading my life. The biggest step was admitting I needed childcare. If I wanted my business to follow the ambitious trajectory I had planned for it, I could no longer run it from home. The expansion needed to be taken seriously and so I had to compromise on my idyllic scenario – cool mumpreneur puts kids first and drives business success – and get real. When I came home, I enrolled the children into summer camp (still only for school hours, so they had their afternoons with me) – and moved the business into a production and retail outlet on a local high street.

At first this seemed like failure and dishonouring my values, but I quickly felt empowered and rejuvenated, and I motored forward even more positively. I was back on my way.

Until the next life jolt…

Double joy

Three years later, The Bespoke Gift Company was four years old, booming and enjoying fabulous publicity, including a slot on ITV's *This Morning*. My son was now six and my daughter four. I had expanded my range, partnered with pioneering retail brands like notonthehighstreet, and was running personalised gift concessions in Debenhams. I was having glittery fun selling tens of thousands of personalised letters from Father Christmas through Tesco, Asda and every other savvy retailer who offered them as a cute add-to-basket check-out option. My creativity was effervescent, my team were my rock and I was about to enter a bold new franchise model, opening gift outlets on ten UK high streets. Then fate made a miraculous intervention: in January 2009 I found out I was pregnant with twins. Twins!

That was news I never ever expected to hear in my lifetime. As I said to the sonographer before falling off the hospital bed: 'Oh. My. God!' OMG indeed. Wow – this was big news! This was almighty, humungous, heaven-sent, divine news. I was ecstatic! Seriously elated, delirious, and could not wipe the gleeful smile off my face. I still can't, in fact. Such a total blessing – or blessings, to be exact...

With this momentous news came another period of reflection and inevitable but necessary planning. I could not manage the business expansion I had envisaged with two young children plus a twin on each hip. Actually, let me rephrase this: I knew my heart and soul were thrilled at the prospect of stepping off my entrepreneurial wheel and throwing myself headlong into twindom for a few years. I was not going to miss out on one precious second of this fragile moment of my rapidly progressing life.

I chose to let the company slide into second place, taking pressure off myself out of respect for our burgeoning little tribe. I chose not to hire a team of growth officers to manage business expansion. I chose to alter any plans which would distract me from my family. I chose to prioritise family over income – an easy choice to make. This was conscious, deliberate decision-making which empowered and excited me as I prepared to return to full-time motherhood for a while. The twins for me represented a heaven-sent opportunity to refocus on what mattered most. As I rationalised it, 'Work will be there forever, but the opportunity to nurture young souls occupies just a tiny fragment of life.' It was liberating to prioritise family over income.

Along they came: Sebastian and Beau, my miraculous twin babies born at home in water in my dimly-lit lounge, one enormous, one tiny, both exquisite in their perfection. And so another new era of my life began. I describe how I survived and thrived during those years of having four children under the age of seven in the 'Energy' chapter. For a start, I took total control of my body in a way that protected me from the ravages of no sleep, breastfeeding twins for fifteen months, and the perpetual domestic demands. I didn't get ill or crack once. To avoid the burnouts I'd had during the early years with my first two cherubs, this time I focused carefully, eliminating every ounce of harmful food and drink, nourishing my soul by being kind to myself whenever the moment presented itself (at last I learned to accept help from willing visitors – even the postman once!) and by upping my spiritual practice (yes, I actually made time for meditation and journaling).

I prioritised ruthlessly: If I needed to rest instead of change the beds to be a better mother later, I rested, and those wretched sheets waited. I had to preserve my own strength, my immune function, my spirit. Embracing self-love amid the chaos was how I flourished in that period, despite the dire predictions of naysayers warning me about the twin hell that was coming. I honestly look back on that first year with the twins as one of the most blessed periods of my life to date. I was happy, purposeful, and grateful every minute of every day. Such a fantastic (if chaotic!) time of life.

Corporate-dom revisited

Fast-forward three years and I've sold The Bespoke Gift Company and been offered the chance to join a local advertising agency to run a new department there. I can still do the school run and I have a cherished family member looking after the twins during the day, so I suddenly find myself no longer a business owner but a cog in a corporate wheel.

It was a tough time emotionally. I was exhilarated by being back in a bustling agency, working with a hugely talented leadership team. But I was devastated to the core of my soul to be away from the children after so many idyllic years combining work and motherhood on my own terms. For ten years I'd never not done the school run both morning and afternoon. I'd never had to ask permission to go to a nativity play or sports day. I'd never been so riddled with guilt over leaving the children.

I cried myself to sleep each night, drove to work sobbing each morning, cried in the toilets at work, and had panic attacks in the middle of the night. On one level, I was all consumed by heartache at leaving the children. On another level, I was invigorated by work. It was a time of intense emotional stress and deep internal conflict.

By day I was a high-performing, positive, achieving agency exec driving business momentum upward, but by night, after my greedy, desperate and joyful reunions with the children, I would collapse into bed heartbroken once more, weeping over the fact that I would have mere moments with the children in the morning before the childminder arrived and I was off on my corporate ladder again.

While I was physically liberated from the burden of four little people's demands each day, the mental, soulful stress took its toll. I was back into 'Binky Burnout' zone again before I knew it: off work for two weeks at a time, with my endlessly concerned parents coming to the rescue. Obviously, I didn't die of heart break and the melodrama of guilty-working-motherhood faded. We all slowly adjusted, until eighteen months later I found myself headhunted to join a major global advertising conglomerate and a different chapter in my working life began. I entered a refreshingly modern, people-centric corporate world where flexible working was encouraged, in experimental pursuit of high performance. I was back to running my schedule on my terms, no mummy guilt required.

AND NOW

So this brings my story up to date. I'm now in another, even more devotedly 'people first', advertising conglomerate, running an innovation business division, which I love. I'm still in a senior leadership position, still driving results, and blessed to be doing so on my terms.

The beauty of where I am today? I am now 100% in balance.

I work flexibly around my family. I organise my time to fit in exercise, my passions and my work goals. I say no when I need to. I am rarely ill. I don't burn out. I don't suffer stress (well only good, energising stress – more on how to embrace that later). I eat well, I sleep well, I think well, I deliver exceptional output and I'm happy. I'm proud of who I am, of what I have achieved and of what I continue to achieve.

I have not got to this point of balance and productivity without learning many lessons along the way. Each time I've collapsed I've picked myself up and taken note of what went wrong, addressed what needed to change, and bit by bit, month by month, year by year I've reached equilibrium. I'm finally living in harmony with my natural state. I preserve myself, consciously and carefully, able to serve my corporation, my family and my customers most effectively. I now wake up and spring up out of bed.

Let me teach you short cuts so you can too. Don't suffer twenty years of floundering around as I did. Don't hurt yourself along the way. Follow the six simple steps in my Energy-SCAPE™ programme and I guarantee you will revitalise your life. You will enhance what is already fabulous with an extra sprinkle of glitter, and you will obliterate anything that is dragging you down with a defiant zap. You will rediscover your sparkle. You will reconnect with the you who may have faded to grey along the way. You will step out of the whirl-wind, down off the treadmill, and take control. Best of all, you'll be doing all of this with a big fat grin on your face and kale juice – or vodka lime soda – in your hand!

CHAPTER ONE: **Energy**
Self-Awareness
Cleanse
Action
Play
Enrichment

> 'The most important thing in life is your inner energy.
> If you're always tired and never enthused, then life is
> no fun. But if you're always inspired and filled with
> energy, then every minute of every day is an exciting
> experience. Learn to work with these things.'
> – Michael A. Singer

I woke groggily from my comatose slumber to the wail of 'mama, mama'. My limbs were lead weights, pinning me beneath the duvet; my brain was foggy, my head heavy, my eyes throbbing with pain as the cries penetrated my dawning consciousness. My toddler twins had woken from their afternoon nap and I was on duty to tend to them. I was off sick from work with yet another bout of flu, so I'd naively cancelled the childminder to save the fee. Alone in the house with the boys, I now needed to swoop into action. I'd snatched a restorative nap while they slept, but as I lay there in my sickbed, I felt far from restored. I was riddled with a virus, exhausted from work overwhelm, and attempting to carry out my parenting duties, but I was seriously floored. I let the wails crawl into my psyche and lolled my aching head towards the window, gazing out at the sky, and I prayed. I prayed to some God, any god, anything, to come and rescue me from this state of incapacity and infuse me with vitality. I prayed for help – for someone to come and clean the house, tend to the children, do the school run, respond to my emails, talk to my customers, iron my clothes, buy the food, cook the dinner, think my thoughts for me. I was utterly spent; to get myself upright and staggering towards their bedroom, where their eager little faces and chubby arms would await me in their tandem cots, took superhuman mental resolve. I was eight days in to yet another major, debilitating, depleted energy crisis. My cycle of burnouts continued…

YOUR PERSONAL ENERGY STOCKTAKE

Before you embark on any path of transformation you need to take stock of where you are now. Ultimately your energy affects your productivity. If your energy is balanced and flowing as it should, you will be Ms Productive, and happily so. If your energy is out of kilter, and you're living in a yo-yo cycle of high performance followed by burnout, the net result is that you're not productive at all. Optimal energy flow should be consistent enough to see you flourishing as a woman, able to seize life as your best self.

Energy is defined as 'the strength and vitality required for sustained physical or mental activity'. For the purposes of this book and empowered womanhood I'm drawing on the Eastern understanding of energy: the Chinese *chi*, the life force. *Chi* is respected and honoured in Chinese medicine, which has itself been widely adopted in Western culture over the past fifty years, with more holistic doctrines like acupuncture entering mainstream practice. 'Alternative' medicine takes the whole being into consideration, approaching body, mind and soul holistically and always investigating the cause, never just treating the symptom. Why, in the UK now we even have a Royal Homeopathic Hospital with referrals available free on the NHS – a huge stride in the Western orthodox understanding of health.

Jing (pronounced 'ying') denotes the inherent energy reserves we are born with and is largely determined by genetics and bio-individuality. Every one of us has a different level of this energy reserve, and you'll see it manifested in bouncy toddlers compared with more placid ones. It's a limited resource that will end when we die of natural causes. A healthy lifestyle can help to replenish and prolong this energy, and sleep is a brilliant example of how to restore and boost it.

Chi, or *qi*, (pronounced 'chee') is the inherent life force and energy in all things, underpinning the exercise principles of Tai Chi and meditative Buddhist mindfulness practice. It flows through and animates the movement of our bodies. It's a fundamental principle of Chinese medicine that when fatigue hits hard, or a plant starts to wilt, the reserves of this energy in the organism have been depleted. Thus equilibrium comes from preserving, boosting and restoring the life force.

Imagine you were about to design a new garden. You'd appraise what you already have to work with, extrinsic and intrinsic factors, and how to plan for optimal visual impact. You'd assess what's set in stone and what's malleable. You'd consider the patio and the lawn, light and shade, and how they will affect what grows. You'd plan modifications to the layout to accommodate your most vibrant vision, taking into account where the best soil is and how to nourish it, what will bloom where, the bio-individuality of each plant and the maintenance it needs. And so it is with ourselves before we effect change in our lives. If you are serious about stepping out of your whirlwind into a place of balance and ful-filment, it absolutely has to begin from within.

You are a beautiful, complex woman made up of body, mind and soul. Blending head and heart, you're a mass of intricate neurological and nervous systems all pulsing, flowing and zinging away to enable you to function optimally always. And that's the real gift. The miracle of life is that we are born blessed with mental and physical faculties that empower us to grow up into this wonderful world as brilliantly as we choose to. We don't have to read an instruction manual to learn to walk, to smile, to love – it's our default setting. As babies we are happy and content most of the time and upset only when our needs aren't met. Abraham

Maslow's hierarchy identifies the basic needs as shelter and food, and, beyond that, love and spiritual realms of connection and enlightenment. Basically, if your nappy needs changing you cry, if you're hungry you cry, if you get a bit lonely without smiles and cuddles you may grizzle, but life is simple and, in the main, joyful.

So what happens as we grow up? The purity of innocently chasing joy and creativity when we play as children starts to fade as the influence of parents, teachers, the media and socialisation begins to instil beliefs and rules about how we should conduct ourselves, which we then accept as normality. Gradually we start to suppress our intuitive way of being to conform. Scientists have found a direct correlation between diminishing creativity and diminishing happiness. Once we stop creating so freely, little pieces of ourselves seem to fade away, to be replaced by an increase in depression, anxiety and a whole lot of self-persecution. By our late teens many of us are privately riddled with fear and apprehension about this big wide world and what role we're going to play in it; it doesn't feel as 'natural' or 'easy' as those fairy stories of our childhoods, now locked away in the dusty loft forever, once suggested.

As part of socialisation we begin to buy into a culture that celebrates high achievement above all else. In institutions from schools to our first work organisations, we witness meritocracies – and linear, conformist ones at that –rewarding those who deliver the highest, best-quality output for whatever the institution deems matters most. (No prizes for best tree climber at primary school.) For us to win at this life malarkey we need to be giving our all, demonstrating our competence, capabilities and positive impact at every moment. Life – and indeed success, it seems – is about proving ourselves, strengthening our strengths, pursuing competition and relentlessly chasing the public accolade of a rosette, a pewter cup, an award, a framed certificate, recognition in some form or other. Seemingly, success needs to be *evidenced* to progress in life, and so the race is on.

Think of a university student and you'll see a picture of the studious intellectual burning the midnight oil over her dissertation. Think of the graduate trainee and you'll see a fresh-faced twenty-something working twelve hours a day in the office, bright and breezy throughout. Think of the TV ad stay-at-home new mother, with her immaculate home and rosy-cheeked cherubs lolling on the deep plush carpet with their sanitised wooden toys (no plastic in this household, of course). The images of success are glamourised, glossy, sheeny-shiny looks at exciting, high-achieving lifestyles.

What these images don't show are the student hungover, mainlining coffee and cigarettes then missing lectures the next day as she's slept late after handing in her paper. The graduate is exhausted and high. The mother is depressed and lonely. These sensationalised, heavily edited media images take no account of the demands of projected high achievement. And that's the fundamental problem: we've all been driving ourselves to achieve social media ideals at the expense of reality.

We've hopped on our life treadmills and worked our little toned butts off to prove to the world that we can do it too, and, look, here's the evidence to prove it – 'Come round for dinner on Saturday, sweetie, why don't you?' But we never consciously address the cost of having it all.

THE ENERGY COMPROMISE

We've chased the dreams and the glory without respecting our own natural energy rhythms. I did it and I suspect you do too. We resist sleep, we artificially stimulate, we glorify our 'busyness' as something to be revered, we keep on going, keep on buzzing: like – like – emoji – emoji – yay to my world – click – click.

Until we crack.

The energy compromise, I believe, starts as early as primary school and is in fact worse than ever today, with the highest number of children in pre- and post-school care ever recorded in the UK, meaning that they have the lowest levels of 'down time' at home ever. Children are pushed to achieve, get good grades, concentrate at school and then jostled into endless after-school clubs, play-dates, holidays – it's all go, go, go from the get-go. What happens to these tired little children who have to keep on keeping on? Well, they certainly don't sleep longer or go to bed earlier. They may start to rely on sugar highs and horrifically they turn to energy drinks (mercifully now on the decline, thanks to new regulations). They start to boost their own energy artificially through external substances. Is it any wonder when, later, alcohol and recreational drugs become so alluring? It's a natural progression, surely, when they've enjoyed years of fake highs already. (Don't get me started on the parents who feed their babies tea, coffee and caffeinated drinks in their bottles…)

If children are denied recharging time because of their packed schedules, it's no wonder we as adults often fail to build relaxation into our daily, weekly or even monthly schedules. Relaxation tends to be comatose recovery rather than deliberate, scheduled rest time.

Alpha femininity – ouch!

Let's take a moment to look at the characteristics of the alpha female before we dive into how to address this energy crisis.

The alpha female gets shit done. She looks great and she wows everyone she meets. She's vivacious, fit, and generally well paid; she loves her career and is respected in her industry; she's running her home as she runs her business, her kids are sorted, her husband happy. Seemingly, she's rocking her world.

Alphas – male or female – enjoy their power: they enjoy decision making, are well aware of the impact of the choices they make, and of how they achieve their goals.

But they also have a tendency to squash – make that obliterate – things that don't enable them to get where they want to go, and that includes 'self-squashing'. Alphas don't waver in pursuit of the end point, and if it means no sleep, no food, no let-up, then so be it. Self is pushed to the bottom of the priority list. Oddly and rather sadly, people are often quite proud of this: 'I don't need sleep, oh no, just coffee all day.' 'My weekend was great, thanks. I was in the office smashing the pitch deck.'

Ugh.

Hearing this sort of thing makes me cringe, but shamefully I hear my own voice echoing in my head. I have snatched a few hours' sleep then been back in the office for 7am, wanting to hit a deadline and impress a boss. I have skipped meals to accommodate work/exercise/ family time. I have bragged about a weekend spent in the office (away from my family, oh, shame on me!). I know I'm not alone. Do you regularly put yourself last and think you're being so clever, so selfless, putting the kids, your boss, your husband, first?

This disrespect for your physical and fundamental needs is so harmful it's essential to examine what happens when we do push ourselves physically, emotionally and mentally to the brink.

IMPROVING YOUR BALANCE

There are six core areas we need to pay attention to if we want to honour our PBS: Productivity Balance System.

1. Sleep – restorative or fitful?

2. Diet – optimal nutrition

3. Fake energy – borrowed stimulants

4. Relaxation – mindful R&R

5. Extreme productivity – over-exercise, overwork, overthinking, overdoing

6. Emotional stress – burdens weighing heavy on our shoulders

---

EXERCISE: YOUR ENERGY SCALE

Score yourself from 1 to 5 on where you sit on the energy scale for each of these key areas, 1 being low and depleted, 5 being high and zingy. Take time out to reflect deeply as you contemplate each area; don't cheat yourself here. The purpose of the exercise is to identify where you need to prioritise the self-love most to shift back into a more balanced state. I recommend keeping a record of your scores in a notebook or journal, so you can look back and monitor your progress.

---

1. Sleep

The healing power of sleep is phenomenal. We revere sleep in my household. Not just from a 'lazy Saturday morning' or 'teenagers lie in bed all day' perspective, but in an 'I have turned my life around by consciously respecting the value of deep sleep' way.

I grew up in the 80s, when the 'work hard, play hard, sleep is for babies' mentality was the status quo. If you were to succeed you didn't want to waste time in bed. Only once motherhood hit and I was well and truly denied sleep did I recognise the profound effects on my mental, emotional and physical abilities. I was literally disabled by tiredness. By the time I had navigated the first year of nursing baby twins around the clock and sunk to a level of ongoing sleep deprivation few people experience (but surging prolactin levels filled me with such endless love in those tender moonlit hours I felt blessed – hormones, eh?), I had misguidedly come to believe I could function on forty minutes' sleep a night. Dangerously, I later took that belief into my work. I remember one night setting my alarm for 2am to do two hours of work before racing back to bed, snatching a couple more hours before the alarm went off again at 6am so I could get my exhausted self back up to London. Even my sleep was adrenaline-filled and had an agenda! And I wondered why I kept burning out…

Only once I studied sleep and recognised the cost of disregarding bedtime did my life start to transform, so

I beseech you to take heed. You can learn how much sleep you need to feel good and think clearly simply by taking note of your own nightly rhythms – how long you sleep for and how much of your sleep is undisturbed – for fourteen consecutive days. You can then use this to identify what triggers your peak daily zing. Personally, I need just over seven hours to feel fabulous.

Interestingly, the hotel chain guru Conrad Hilton was famed for his deep reverence for sleep. He recognised the rejuvenating power of sleep, both physically and cognitively, and would often make time slap bang in the middle of the day for a nap. If he had a major decision to make, he would draw his office black-out curtains, lock his door, lie down and literally 'sleep on it' for however long he needed, so he could shift from his conscious to his unconscious mind to allow the solution to rise to the surface.

Some of the major restorative functions of the body, from muscle growth and tissue repair to protein synthesis, occur mostly, or in some cases *only*, during sleep. If you ever see someone looking like the 'walking dead', they are visual proof of the effects of lack of sleep. Their cells haven't been given the opportunity to rejuvenate, replenish and evolve. Make sure that isn't you.

Sleep is sacred. It is your healing time. It is your moment to rejuvenate, restore and re-energise ready for the next day.

What to do

Create a haven: Make sure your bedroom is a sleep sanctuary. Ensure your mattress, pillows, duvet and even sheets make you feel totally wonderful. Personally, I love to feel as though I'm sleeping on a cloud, so I have a four-inch foam topper on top of my mattress. (Princess that I am!) I'm also a huge fan of The White Company's bedding and treat myself during sale time to their highest thread-count Egyptian cotton bedding every couple of years. It's a divine treat sliding into bed each evening and my bedroom truly is my favourite relaxation space.

Beware the blue light: Avoid screens as you wind down before sleep. Our devices emit light of all colours, but it's the blues in particular that pose a danger to sleep. Blue light prevents the release of melatonin, a hormone associated with night-time tranquillity that reduces alertness and makes sleep more inviting. Halting production of melatonin means you're inhibiting your gentle descent into slumber. I refuse to have a television in my bedroom, I have to be ill to work on my laptop in bed, and I switch my phone to airplane mode and place it on the floor before I go to sleep. Beware: teenagers with bedrooms resembling NASA's control centre have the worst possible conditions for deep, rejuvenating sleep, so change this if you can.

Soak in an aromatherapy bath: Scents have power to evoke emotions and memories instantly and can directly affect our bodies through our nervous system.

It is the olfactory nerve, which starts from our nose and enters the skull through tiny holes to connect directly to the brain, that gives us our sense of smell. This nerve rapidly sends signals to many different parts of the brain, including the limbic system and amygdala, which are in charge of emotions, mood and memory. These systems are also in charge of regulating our autonomic nervous system, which can either trigger a fight-or-flight response or can soothe us by turning on the para-sympathetic nervous system, which relaxes our bodies. This explains why scents can so quickly stimulate phys-ical reactions in our bodies and have lasting effects after their source is gone. Essential oils like lavender have even been shown to act in the same way that anti-anxiety medications do on certain neuroreceptors.

Aromatherapy is a complementary medicine practice that taps into the healing power of scents from essential oils to balance your mind, body and spirit. Essential oils can be diluted with water and diffused into the air, or a few drops can be gently rubbed into acupressure points on the body. Studies have shown that specific essential oils can help relieve stress, relax the body and promote better sleep; these are:

- Lavender
- Ylang-ylang
- Bergamot
- Lemon
- Clary sage
- Jasmine

No food after 8pm: If food is fuel why on earth do you need fuel as your body begins to shut down for the day? Personally, I stick to eating for energy, snacking continuously throughout the day when my energy dips, making lunch my biggest meal and dinner light and as early as possible. I totally understand work commitments may get in the way of this, so try at least to be mindful of what's best for your body and mind, and see if you can bring dinner forward when possible.

After a meal your body is in digestion mode, which means it's working, it's stimulated, it's producing gastric acids, and still alert and functioning, which hinders sleep. Your stomach should be resting and recuperating along with your brain. Eating late also causes triglyceride levels to rise, which signals to the body that it needs to store fat ready to produce energy when required. You don't need that energy so the fat produced stays in the body as weight gain. We tend to graze and snack in the evening, too, as part of our end-of-the-day comfort, despite already being full, which exacerbates the weight gain further.

Read: It's heaven to dive into the pages of a book and escape the day. Deliberately detach your mind from work, the kids, the house and trigger your imagination, snuggle up and lose yourself.

Silence: Savour peace and quiet. Enjoy the spiritual growth that blooms amid silence. Tune into yourself. Listen to your intuition. Switch everything off and just be.

Reflection: Choose a winding-down routine that works for you. Build in time at the end of each day to become present and still, by whatever means. I write a journal every night without fail before sleep. Writing is my therapy. I let my thoughts flow, I reflect on the day, I observe what I did well, what I could have done better; I consider what the next day holds, what I'm grateful for and who I send love to. It's a ritual I've had since I was eight years old and for me a day isn't complete without putting pen to paper. Create whatever feels right for you. (Find more inspiration in the 'Enrichment' chapter later.)

2. Diet

We're suffering an epidemic of tragic proportions through our Western diet. Obesity and heart disease rates have reached, quite literally, heart-breaking levels. In the United Kingdom we actually have to build extra-large, robust ambulances to collect overweight patients in trouble. The diet industry globally is worth a staggering $245bn per year. Food has never been so accessible, abundant and diverse, but industrialisation has shifted us into a world of processed foodstuffs far from their original form. It's no surprise that we have seen a chronic rise in allergies, immune diseases, 'brain' maladies in children from autism to ADHD, an alarming and increasing volume of pharmaceutical dependencies, and alcohol addiction.

There's an emerging science connecting gut and cognitive function. In her book, *Gut and Psychology*

Syndrome, Dr Natasha Campbell-McBride evidences how conditions such as ADHD and autism disappear when the intestinal tract is 'healed' through natural foods. Similarly, in his book *Brain Grain: The Surprising Truth about Wheat, Carbs, and Sugar – Your Brain's Silent Killers*, Dr David Perlmutter states, 'We're going to explore what happens when the brain is bombarded by carbohydrates, many of which are packed with inflammatory ingredients like gluten that can irritate your nervous system. The damage can begin with daily nuisances like headaches and unexplained anxiety and progress to more sinister disorders such as depression and dementia.' The medical industry is paying attention as more and more trials prove that the body and mind can be restored to optimal states with an unprocessed diet.

The 'alternative' health movement regularly laments our increasing toxic overload. We may not be able to control air pollution, but we can respect our livers and avoid stressing this delicate, critical organ. Mortality due to liver disease (of which cirrhosis is the end state) is increasing more than any other chronic condition in the UK.

The liver's primary task is to aid elimination from the body by converting waste into urine. Primeval man needed the liver for efficient bodily function and to cope with the odd crisis, be it poisonous berries or bacteria-ridden meat. Today our livers are acutely stressed most of the time.

The main culprit, in my humble opinion, is the devil that is white sugar. And I'm not just worried about the impact of sugar rotting our teeth, I'm worried about the long-term consequences of the burden of sugar on our physiology. I have endless debates, or rather full-blown arguments, with my teenage son over sugar. He's adamant that it's not as harmful as I make out. I tell him it's his addiction speaking…!

Refined, white sugar is not a food substance; it's a chemical which stimulates a dopamine response. Since dopamine contributes to feelings of pleasure and satisfaction as part of our reward system, this neurotransmitter plays a dominant part in addiction by creating cravings. Sugar robs our bodies of nutrients and weakens our immune systems – see *That Sugar Film* for a brilliant Aussie experiment in which Damon Gameau spends six weeks eating sugary foods with full medical supervision. It's harrowing how quickly his body starts to succumb to fatty liver disease.

As William Duffy states in his bestselling book, *Sugar Blues*, 'Sugar is nothing but a chemical. They take the juice of the cane or the beet and they refine it to molasses and then they refine it to brown sugar and finally to strange white crystals' – a process that he directly compares to the production of heroin from the juice of the poppy.

This poison lurks in the most innocent-looking foods, from fresh tomato pasta sauces to 'healthy' yoghurts to breads. It's the number one reason we suffer such extreme daily energy surges, dips, then more chronic fatigue.

Sarah Wilson, author of *I Quit Sugar*, tells us about the impact eliminating sugar had on her moods, explaining that when she first quit sugar, she treated it as an invitation to try out a new way of living, just to see how it went. Her health was transformed in a matter of weeks: 'I experienced a mood change. Actually, more accurately, it was a mood stabilisation. Since quitting sugar I've sensed a steady, calm happiness that has previously eluded me.'

Eliminating sugar (not natural sugars such as lactose, found in milk, and fructose, in fruit, but the glucose in processed food that causes blood sugar spikes) is what I attribute the magical transformation of my immune system to. To boot there was the fantastic impact on my physique: within a few weeks of carefully cutting the white stuff from my diet, not only did I feel like a sprightly twenty-year-old again, but I had shed every unwanted squidgy bit of my body. It was an immediate – and most welcome – side-effect.

I must warn you that the withdrawal period can be pretty intense. For me (and I didn't think I had a 'bad' diet beforehand) the detoxification period was tough. I suffered a few days of flu-like symptoms and swollen lymph glands. I was sleeping from the moment the children were in bed, for twelve deep, healing hours, yet still waking heavy-limbed and achy. But as the sugar loosened its poisonous grip on my insides I started to bloom like a liberated butterfly. I felt lighter, more youthful, and alive. It was so exciting to feel my natural vigour returning. Give it a go; I promise you won't regret it.

The other radical change I made, which I believe has also contributed to my vitality, is to adopt a high-alkaline diet. I mainly eat greens – and raw greens at that. I love vegetable juices, and avocados are my daily staple. It's not just greens, though, that are high alkaline: delights such as watermelon also tick this box.

An alkaline diet:

- Protects bone density and muscle mass
- Lowers the risk of hypertension and stroke
- Lowers chronic pain and inflammation
- Boosts vitamin absorption and prevents magnesium deficiency
- Helps improve immune function and protects against cancer
- Can help you maintain a healthy weight

The best sources of alkaline are:

- **Fresh fruits and vegetables:** These promote alkalinity the most; some of the top picks include mushrooms, citrus, dates, raisins, spinach, grapefruit, tomatoes, avocado, summer black radish, alfalfa grass, barley grass, cucumber, kale, wheat grass, broccoli, oregano, garlic, ginger, green beans, endive, cabbage, celery, red beet, watermelon, figs and ripe bananas.

- **Raw foods:** Ideally you should consume a good proportion of your food raw, as cooking foods depletes their alkalising minerals; try juicing or lightly steaming fruit and vegetables.
- **Plant proteins:** Almonds, navy beans, lima beans and most other beans are good choices.
- **Alkaline water:** This is water that's less acidic than regular tap water, with a pH of nine to eleven; distilled water is fine to drink and water filtered with a reverse osmosis filter is slightly acidic, but still a far better option than tap water or purified bottled water. Adding pH drops, lemon or lime juice, or baking soda to your water can also boost its alkalinity.
- **Green drinks:** Drinks made from green vegetables and grasses in powder form are loaded with alkaline-forming foods and chlorophyll; chlorophyll is structurally similar to our own blood and helps alkalise the blood.

The personal benefit of adding considerably more alkalinity to my diet? My skin glows, my nails are so strong you'd struggle to snap them and – hooray, hooray – my hair has started to thicken up again.

I notice now that when I eat sugary snacks or a chemical-laden, processed dinner, the next day I have bloodshot eyes, rather like waking with a hangover. This is evidence of a straining liver triggered into out-of-the-ordinary elimination. I'll always pay attention to signs like these. If you get a furry tongue and bleary eyes, check over what you ate the previous day and consciously experiment with elimination trials.

Fundamentally, eat for nourishment and trust your instinct. If something 'feels' so far from its natural state that your intuitive reaction to it is that it is failing to nourish your mind, body and soul, reject it and find something else. It is definitely wise to embrace intuitive eating. A good tip is to pause at the fridge door, close your eyes, become present, breathe and deeply consider what you actually want. Quite often your body will say mango over the chocolate digestive. Try it.

Evelyn Tribole, author of *Intuitive Eating*, encourages us to avoid obsessive, faddy restriction and defines healthy eating as 'having a healthy balance of foods and having a healthy relationship with food'. As my mother always says, 'A little bit of what you fancy does you good!' I encourage you to experiment until you find a nutrient-dense diet that makes you feel vibrant, not denied. If you want that cake/gin/ice cream/insert-your-favourite-indulgence once in a while, have it!

Finally, a note on the importance of keeping yourself hydrated: your body is composed of about 60% water. The functions of your bodily fluids include digestion, absorption, circulation, creation of saliva, transportation of nutrients, and maintenance of body temperature – pretty important stuff, so it's vital to keep the water levels in your body balanced. Drink water lots. Drink lots of water. Drink, drink, drink.

I drink pints and pints of water during the day and am never without a bottle of water in my bag, on my desk, by my bed. In fact, my hydration starts with my ritual first pint, which I gulp down as I embrace the day. I visualise the water cascading through my body waking up every cell, invigorating me for optimum performance throughout the day. (See more about my morning routine in the 'Cleanse' chapter.)

What to do

Cut out refined white sugar, eat a predominantly alkaline diet abundant with fresh fruits and vegetables, hydrate and trust your intuition.

3. Fake energy

It's pretty damned obvious that when you rob Peter to pay Paul it's going to come back and slap you in the face. You're not solving anything.

The perpetual 'achieve then break, achieve then break, achieve then break' cycle that so many women are locked into today is actually only made possible by fake energy. We borrow energy from artificial stimulants that keep us pepped up and going despite our bodies telling us otherwise.

Think of the last time you had a cold. Did you nestle in bed with a homemade vegetable soup or hot lemon and ginger tea and sleep it off as your body was gagging for you to do? Nope, you'll have whacked out the Lemsip, consuming caffeine, phenylalanine, sugars, paracetamol and whatever other concoction of chemicals lie hidden in that toxic remedy, so you could get up and out of bed and back on your life slog. What's the betting you didn't just make it out on the school run and to the office but still did your lunchtime run and client drinks in the evening? You kept on keeping on, despite your body saying pleeeeaaaase stop.

When did you last wake up on a Saturday morning and roll over for a snooze to recover gently from the pace of the week? In fact, did you jump up with the kids, make a fresh pot of filter coffee, and zip out the door to their sports clubs – a start as pacey as a usual week day?

And last Friday night, as you finished up for the week, did you slope contentedly home to curl up with a book in your PJs or did you find Prosecco energy from nowhere to see you out dancing till dawn with your girlfriends?

We're in an era where it's okay to push on through. It's acceptable to ignore your body's natural rhythms and suppress your own fatigue with artificial stimulants. It's the norm. Get up, then get down with medicated sleeping tablets.

Just look at the energy drink market. Sales continue to increase year on year globally, with brands like Red

Bull becoming household names and selling over six billion cans per year worldwide. And let's not ignore those children hopping around (bizarrely proudly) brandishing their ADHD labels before anyone bothered to check their stash of bloodline Dr Pepper under the bed. It's apparently cool to buzz off fake energy. Hey, you could even become a rocket man (one of Red Bull's most notorious stunts). These drinks (or powders) aren't just laced with caffeine, they tend to include additional 'energy boosts' from taurine to guarana – a heady mix of artificial adrenaline.

It's no wonder we're so out of kilter with how we feel in ourselves. Which way does our body want us to go? Up and on with life and our commitments despite the fatigue, or slowly, gently, down as our energy fades naturally.

I got into a coffee and sleeping tablet cycle. I managed to get (alpha female victory as I saw it then) hormone-related prescription sleeping tablets: 'Oh doctor, I can't sleep just before my period, please help me.' I then used these to help me 'come down' after intense days fuelled by coffee highs. When I needed ultra-productivity, so I could, for example, accommodate my corporate demands with the children's needs and the household chores, or tackle an eye-watering task list that no human without super powers could cope with, coffee, coffee, coffee lifted me up and into blitzing through sixteen-hour days with élan. Then I'd crash into bed, brain still whirling, whirring, twizzled with ideas and plans and no desire to settle. Enter the powerful sedatives and a deep, false sleep. Alarm clock off at 6am and away we go again. I would literally sip my cup of coffee knowing that I'd be taking a tablet again that night. If I'd run out of tablets I wouldn't have a coffee.

Interestingly, when I confronted the ultimate physical endurance test of juggling four children under the age of seven while breastfeeding newborn twins and keeping a home and business ticking along, I knew there was no room for caffeine in my life. I nourished myself with juices, soups and zero caffeine as I couldn't risk being twitchy during the only forty-minute sleep window I might have on any given night. There was no time to dabble with artificial ups and downs; I had to be there for my children to the best of my ability, so I took my energy management seriously. It worked, and I wasn't ill and didn't crack once throughout that entire period.

Back at the coalface several years later I was more focused on work than on the children, or indeed myself, and lo and behold I slipped back into a cycle of caffeine and sleeping tablets once again. Only after another episode of critical immune breakdown did I consider breaking the pattern. Goodbye caffeine and, funnily enough, goodbye sleeping tablets. I've never looked back.

I'm equally sensitive to alcohol. It's easy to feel as if you're bolstering your energy reserves with a glass of something intoxicating. Last night was a typical Friday night: end-of-the-week exhaustion had set in but we needed to pack up the car for six of us ready to get out of the door and on the road to Chamonix by 6am. Where to get the energy? Prosecco for me, beer for my husband. Fake energy.

It's so easy to slip into this flow. Society permits it. Society actually encourages it. But if you are to take control of your energy, you need to be aware of your own patterns here.

What to do

Make a list of what you ingested/took/did over the past week that artificially elevated your energy levels: at work, at home, at play. Examine foods, drugs, alcohol, and caffeinated drinks (check the ingredients of your fizzy favourites). Look at when you gave in, when you needed it most, and what the impact was.

Consider what would happen if you abandoned these crutches. What would your life look like if you were in step with your natural rhythm? How would you feel if you responded to your body's pleas to stop? Could you?

4. Relaxation

Relaxation is low on the priority list for a high percentage of the Western population. Our high-functioning selves assume that there's no time for down time and certainly not for 'me time'. We wait until we collapse before we stop.

I used to fall asleep in the dentist's chair. No kidding. I was so happy to be having a filling and to know that no one would be asking anything of me for twenty full minutes that I could drift off. What a signal this was of a life out of kilter!

Can you relate to this? What happens to you if you stop for a moment? At the hairdresser? In the nail salon? Reading bedtime stories to your children? I'll bet as soon as you pause and allow yourself to relax momentarily the waves of exhaustion hit and you feel the swoon of sleep descending invitingly. Oh, the effort to drag yourself up off the bed to kiss the children goodnight, then start cleaning the kitchen, prepping school bags for the morning, before responding to the emails you didn't get to during your working day. Oh, I feel your pain – I have absolutely been there!

I openly admit, I've only really learned how to relax in the past few years.

For me, it's not about watching TV or getting drunk or even being with people. For me rejuvenation of body, mind and soul happens alone, privately, in my own space, in my own way. The relaxation routine that sees me end most days contentedly is a lavender and sea salt bath in dimmed lights, followed by journaling in bed before reading, then drifting off to sleep with a self-hypnosis or meditation audio. It's how I detach from the whirl of the day, how I free and cleanse my mind in preparation for tomorrow. But that's just me. We should each build routines that incorporate what we individually know is necessary for our personal inner replenishment.

I make it known to the family that for me to serve them and flourish in life I need time alone and ask that they respect it. Equally, I encourage all of my family members to establish their own rituals so we can respect one another's. I hope the foundations my little ones are building now will set them on the way of balance and fulfilment in the future.

I discuss meditation and self-hypnosis in this section as I've only recently categorised them as relaxation. I actually came to self-hypnosis in my teens as a way of packing in more learning. Why waste sleep when you could be learning another language/life perspective/ how to get better posture? Now I see these techniques as far more sacred than just a way of absorbing French tutorials in my sleep – as mental conditioning rather than aids to subconscious recall. My repository of subliminal audio treats ranges from visualising goals, to eradicating limiting beliefs, to chakra clearing with Kundalini (yoga-influenced) meditation and more. I'm still using my down time to progress areas of my life, but this mental focus is entirely restorative. It is spiritually uplifting and cleansing, and I would never go without it.

Neuroscientists have discovered evidence that mindfulness meditation causes changes in the structure and function of the brain regions involved in the regulation of attention, emotion and self-awareness. Through meditation you can actually rewire your brain to become a better you. *The Huffington Post* cites eight ways meditation can improve your life:

1. It reduces stress

2. It improves concentration

3. It encourages a healthy lifestyle

4. It increases self-awareness

5. It increases happiness

6. It increases acceptance of what is

7. It slows aging

8. It benefits cardiovascular and immune health

To these I would add that it enables creativity and reduces anxiety.

I also love how meditation forces us to slow down and become conscious of our own breathing. The power of breathing, and especially of deep breathing, is essential in our world, where we constantly proclaim, 'I don't have time to breathe!' Slow, deep breathing is the foundation of yogic practice, Buddhist meditation and, from a more practical physical perspective, it boosts lymphatic drainage. (More on the cleansing benefits of deep breathing in the 'Cleanse' chapter.)

What to do

Identify what relaxes and rejuvenates you the most.

Consider people, things, places, habits and environments. List them all and think about ways you can introduce more of them into your daily life.

Are there behaviours you could modify? Is there time you could use specifically for relaxation?

When you chunk your life into daily, weekly, monthly and yearly sections, what are the relaxation moments you would like to invite into your life? How can you build these in more rigidly?

5. Extreme productivity

An all-too-common energy crime committed by modern women every day is one of extreme productivity. We care an awful lot about making a tremendous impact at whatever we turn our hands to, whether it's working out and sculpting that dream body, or rapid career progression, outpacing male (and female) colleagues along the way. Even motherhood can become an area where we study, obsess, practice, perfect and diarise every step of the way. For overachievers, even meditation can become a rigorous month-long stay in a Thai monastery instead of just ten minutes on the Headspace app on the morning commute.

Extreme productivity is something we high-achieving women are proud to have burnt into our psyches. We almost don't notice that we're extreme. We consider it part of our life's plan. Of course we will succeed. We will master it. We will do it – do it until we're in unconscious competence and it's another string to our ever-expanding bow.

Unconscious competence is a desirable state to be in. It's that wonderful state in which you're doing something brilliantly without even realising you're doing it. Driving is a great example of this. Initially, as you learn, you're in patient, gruelling conscious incompetence, actively practising the theory you've learned, faltering over each gear change with furrowed brow as you try, try, try. As you start to master the car as an extension of your own body and mind, you shift into conscious competence, and then eventually hit the lovely state of unconscious control, where you drive automatically, with little brain power needed.

This latter state is the dream. Your cognitive load is lessened. You don't need to think about what you're doing; it just happens. You have freed your brain and made space for new thoughts and to master new skills.

Alpha females know innately that we want to be in a space of unconscious competence. We know that we always want more capacity in our brains. This is what drives us into extreme productivity. It's a form of chasing efficiency. We do the thing that feels good and achieves the results we want over and over again until it happens automatically. Once we've mastered it, we can move on to the next big shiny new life challenge.

When we're in flow and this is happening as part of a balanced life: fantastic! We are the superwomen of our generation. But all too often we trip headlong into frantic productivity through social conditioning born of competitiveness and goal obsession, with abominable disregard for other areas of our lives. It's also a way of hiding from emotional stress. We often enter a hyper-productive state when there is something deep inside we're choosing not to acknowledge, be it subconsciously or consciously. We do it despite the fact that we're potentially breaking ourselves, often reaching a somewhat frenzied state of overproduction that yields harmful results.

Look at the obsessive runner back on her half-marathons before her post-baby ligaments have returned to their pre-baby state. Watch the aspiring managing director working fourteen-hour hour days in pursuit of that promotion and missing a year of her children's lives. Spot the lover-obsessed divorcee unable to concentrate on her work while she moons and overanalyses. Overdoing and overthinking are classic traits of the energy-imbalanced woman.

Dame Helena Morrissey, OBE, author of *Good Time to Be a Girl*, states that developing a great career is not the same as passing an exam. 'There is no test date. No objective assessment. No certificate. There are relationships to navigate and risks to be taken, failures that will inevitably be incurred as well. We need to prepare young women for that.'

She explains that although learning to deal with failure is particularly difficult for girls, whose fear of failure is often stronger than boys', it is an essential skill.

So: how to drop the perfectionism and tune into a gentler way of being? If we're serious about having it all without cracking, we simply have to accept that our definition of 'all' needs some serious thought. True productivity is in fact about careful prioritisation and mindful focus.

What to do

A quiet mind is crucial here. It takes serious self-reflection and observation even to recognise that you're in a damaging state of overproduction. Often it will take a friend or family member (in my case, it's always been my mother) to point out that you're behaving a little too obsessively over this one thing. To cure extreme productivity, deep self-awareness is essential.

For now, what springs to mind as you read this section? Is there any area of your life – be it a thought, person, behaviour or otherwise – you feel you could turn down the pressure on? Be honest and make a note, as we'll be taking this through into your self-awareness work in the next step on our Energy-SCAPE™ journey.

6. Emotional stress

We take a lot on, we women trying to have it all. From family, to home, to work, to perfecting our glossy ideals, we put an awful lot on our feminine shoulders in pursuit of apparently successful lives, apparent best selves. The impact of emotional stress on our bodies, minds and souls inevitably takes its toll.

Physiologically, the outcome of stress is a weakened immune system and accelerated signs of aging, never mind underperformance in our day-to-day lives. You know how people say 'you could see the lines of stress etched on her face'? It's true. Stress is aging. Stressed-out individuals show it from the inside out – think wrinkles, hair loss, weight loss and saggy, black circles under the eyes. And if it's that obvious externally, it doesn't take a genius to consider the internal havoc also at play.

Today, laughter therapy is growing in popularity as a cure for depression and even as a cancer treatment. Laughter decreases stress hormones and increases immune cells and infection-fighting antibodies, thus improving resistance to disease. Laughter triggers the release of endorphins, the body's natural feel-good chemicals. Endorphins promote an overall sense of wellbeing and are even proven to relieve pain temporarily. Laughter is energising. You lift up and vibrate electrically when you are giggling; the world becomes vibrant as you become vibrant in it. Build laughter into your life as an essential.

Of course, rolling around in fits and temporary states of heightened happiness don't take away the stresses and strains in your life that have been creating any energy imbalance. You'll still be in your unhappy marriage, your challenging job, your sleep-deprived new baby zone. You'll be drained and low again when your mind turns back to whatever initially put you in that negative, emotionally stressed state.

This is where perspective comes in. Your beliefs around what is happening to you can either constrict you or free you. You can choose your attitude and indeed what you focus on. Likewise, you can liberate yourself through decision, be it a decision to change your perspective or to take action. More on this in subsequent chapters.

> '*Where focus goes, energy flows.*'
> – Anthony Robbins

To go back to those examples, you can leave your marriage if you're that unhappy or you can focus on the great bits; you can leave your job or use it for personal growth; you can complain about the sleepless nights or you can exalt in your precious babymoon. It's ultimately up to you to take control in ways that energise rather than deplete you.

What to do

Make sure you build in lots of lovely laughter time with your favourite people, TV shows, books and so on. I also urge you to read Eckhart Tolle's *The Power of Now*. Yes, Tolle is a spiritual teacher, and his work may not resonate with you but a perspective that encourages you to silence your chattering mind and shed your emotional burdens simply by becoming present is a gift I can't recommend highly enough. I listen to this audio book whenever I feel overwhelmed. I regain an outlook that is neither saddled with regret over the past, nor frightened by a projected future. I return safely to the present moment and feel lighter, calmer, happier, and devoid of emotional stress. *The Power of Now* teaches you the art of becoming conscious. Open your mind and give it a try…

> 'Grant me the serenity to accept the things I cannot change, courage to change the things I can, and wisdom to know the difference.'
> – Reinhold Niebuhr

CHAPTER TWO: **Self-Awareness**

Energy

Cleanse

Action

Play

Enrichment

*'If your emotional abilities aren't in hand, if you don't
have self-awareness, if you are not able to manage
your distressing emotions, if you can't have empathy
and have effective relationships, then no matter how
smart you are, you are not going to get very far.'*
– Daniel Goleman

My daughter lay face down on her bed, her diminutive body shaking with sobs. Twelve years old
and crushed, she silently willed the world around her to
dissolve. I perched on the duvet alongside her, stroking
her quivering back, tortured with the maternal plight of
wanting to absorb her pain. On she wept, releasing the
pent-up anxiety and sadness of having endured another
school day at the hands of destructive bullies. Her public stoicism evaporated, melting into a virulent stream
of tears, as she embraced the privacy of her bedroom.
Then a stillness came. She flipped over suddenly and sat

up, locking eyes with me, tears halting. Her crumpled physique gained a straight-backed defiance and she announced, 'I feel so sorry for them. They are wasting their lives on me. They can't ever get today back and they've spent it finding ways to humiliate me. I feel so sorry for them. I can't also waste my day. I'm not going to cry any more Mummy. I'm not going to think about this anymore. I'm going to send them loving thoughts and hope they get bored of me really soon.'

If my tenderness towards my daughter had been flowing as I rubbed her back, it gushed in torrents as she spoke these words. The wisdom from such a young soul took my breath away. The inner transformation she'd just experienced. The mental clarity to reframe a situation, to observe her own emotions in a way that enabled her to release the pain and shift into a new state of positive calm. It was a privilege to witness and such a beautiful, touching demonstration of the power of self-awareness. I was in awe. She was enlightened.

If you intend to make any change to your life, to yourself, to your impact on the world, the change must always start from within. Anyone, anywhere, can initiate change by applying the words of Mahatma Gandhi: 'Be the change you want to see in the world.' And so, if you want to put your best self forward, if you want to flourish, start by looking inside.

In my loft are stacks of wicker baskets piled high with journals I've been writing since I was eight, from the sweet padlocked Victoria Plum diaries of my childhood, to the A4 sticker-encrusted books of my teens, through to pastel suede pink or blue journals from my baby-moons. I've captured my life, my feelings, my adventures, my worries, my highs and lows, year after year. I've always connected to writing as my therapy (and, yes, I've dabbled in creative writing and produced cringe-worthy poetry too!). Writing for me has become a form of spiritual practice, a release. These moments of private reflection help me organise the events of my world and explore my feelings more deeply. I close every day with a burst of writing, however tired or short of time I may be.

In *Life's Companion*, Christina Baldwin describes the art of journaling as a spiritual practice. Having written daily for more than fifty years, she encourages us to do the same: 'Millions of people are joined in the knowledge that writing brings insight and calm in the same way that prayer, meditation or a long walk in the woods do. They have discovered that writing allows the racing mind to move at the pace of pen and paper or the pace of typing on the waiting screen – that journal writing *is* a spiritual practice.'

And so it is for me too. My daily writing has expanded my perspectives, enabled me to grow more consciously into purposeful living, and never let one moment slip away uncherished, or at least unnoticed. When I've felt burdened by the intensity of the million pressures and demands on me – all ostensibly urgent – I've paused, downed tools and escaped to my journal for quiet reflection. Just yesterday, after a 6am workout, a 7am school run, an 8am conference call, hundreds of blinking phone notifications, and a gapless meeting schedule for the rest of the day, I needed ten minutes of time out before I set off for my commute into London. My heart was racing, I could feel frenetic thoughts swirling: I was slipping into neurological and physiological chaos. So I grabbed my journal and a camomile tea, sat outside on my carved tree-stump chair in the autumn sunshine and wrote for ten minutes: ten minutes in nature, ten minutes of free-flowing words on paper, ten minutes of solitude. Afterwards, I was grounded, renewed and reinvigorated, ready to thrust back into the day, but more calmly. Creating the space to write is rather like a power nap for the soul.

The fact that I've always journaled made me believe I was very self-aware. I felt I already had the necessary keys to personal development and growth, but it was only when I kept on breaking and suffering burnout after burnout that I realised I needed to go deeper. I needed more of a macro view of my life, beyond the 'should have expressed myself differently today, will try this tomorrow' reflections. I needed to take stock of why I was doing what I was doing in the first place. I needed to assess how what I was thinking was affecting my behaviours, feelings and the results I was achieving.

To the outside world I was doing fabulously – indeed, I epitomised the flourishing woman: a beautiful family, successful business, idyllic home, plentiful friends, fitness, health, zing and so on – but beneath the glossy surface there was chronic stress, cortisol-fuelled productivity and an almost critically strained immune system. I was not flourishing.

I entered a period where I gradually began to question the myth that it's cool to be busy. I had always loved answering 'how are you?' with a long list of my off-the-scale busyness: 'Well, the kids are doing x, the business is growing by y, I'm now running twice a day, yes, yes I'd love a bender this weekend, etc.' I thought I was exuding success. And then I read *The E-Myth* by Michael Gerber, a guide for entrepreneurs, and learned about the idiocy of treading water, of not focusing on the most important things each day, of the danger of not using your personal strengths to best effect, and I started to change the way I ran my business. I hired staff I could delegate the administrative elements to, or the tasks that were not my forte, so I could focus on doing the things I was brilliant at. Within a short time, I was doing less but achieving more. Business was booming. I was working smarter not harder. Genius – or blatantly obvious to anyone on the outside. But that's the challenge: when you're caught up in the maelstrom on the inside it's hard to get perspective.

Alan Sugar once snarled on an episode of *The Apprentice*, 'You're all busy fools!' and it struck such a chord with me. I had been a headless chicken busting a gut without organised focus. But I had turned my chaotic work realm around by strategising, prioritising and seizing purposeful control. I decided to experimentally apply these professional changes to my personal life. And so began one of my deepest periods of self-reflection and a renewed vigour in exploring myself, my values, my beliefs, and my personal energy rhythms to create my unique recipe for life success. It was time for me to understand what triggered burnout and how to prevent it once and for all.

EXERCISE: ARE YOU TOO BUSY TO BREATHE?

I have a dear friend who was referred by her doctor to a specialist to help her breathe – I'm not kidding. She was advised that her pace of life was so frenetic that she was losing her ability to take deep, full, restorative breaths. She needed to re-learn how to breathe properly into her diaphragm to restore physiological equilibrium to her body. Don't let this be you.

Try this 'belly breathing' exercise any time you need to relax or relieve stress. It's easy to do and very restorative.

1. Sit or lie flat in a comfortable position
2. Put one hand on your stomach, just below your ribs and the other hand on your chest
3. Take a deep breath in through your nose, and let your abdomen push your hand out; your chest should not move
4. Breathe out through pursed lips as if you were whistling; feel the hand on your stomach go in, and use it to push all the air out
5. Do this breathing three to ten times, taking your time with each breath
6. Notice how you feel at the end of the exercise

Fundamentally, learn that it is not only acceptable but essential to slow down and breathe. Build taking time out to slow your pace and breathe deeply into your daily routine.

WHY DOES SELF-AWARENESS MATTER SO MUCH?

As I was researching this book I was buoyed, and not particularly surprised, to discover that the personal development genre continues to buck diminishing book publishing trends and grow globally year on year. The world is crying out for help on how to thrive, not just survive. We love our technology-propelled world, but we're struggling to find meaning, satisfaction and happiness in it. Whether we're after spiritual counsel, anthologies of inspirational quotes, or self-help guidance on subjects ranging from work to health, to beauty, to parenting, we're all on a mission to discover how to be and – most importantly – to *feel* better. When we introduced mindfulness training sessions at work the spaces were fully booked within thirty minutes. Even my bank now has soothing sounds of serene birdsong and trickling water instead of hold music. There's a swathe of change afoot for sure.

Scientists have proved that the benefits of deep self-awareness include, but are not limited to:

- Self-control
- The ability to act consciously rather than react passively

- Good psychological health
- A positive outlook on life
- Greater depth of life experience
- Greater compassion for yourself and others

So why on earth don't we all automatically embrace self-awareness? Why don't we carve out time for it in our daily lives? Why does the ego resist inner work? Despite prolific streams of media chatter, bountiful resources and endless events teaching the art of personal development, there remains a disproportionate lack of individual commitment to self-awareness based on the following:

- We claim not to have enough time for self-reflection
- We are not actually present or 'conscious' enough to reflect
- We operate with autopilot as a default setting
- We have a cognitive bias towards 'things always being this way'
- We see self-awareness as self-indulgent or as too selfish
- We resist feedback: 'My way is the right way'

… and so on.

We just don't value the transformational power of self-awareness. Yet in my personal experience it is the only way to truly grow and redefine success on your terms. You have to do the inner work before you can expect any outer results. That's just how it is. As esteemed spiritual guru Deepak Chopra states, 'People need to know that they have all the tools within themselves.'

HOW TO DEVELOP AND MAINTAIN SELF-AWARENESS

Here are some steps to introduce into daily living to encourage gentle, perpetual growth. Choosing one or some of the habits below will start to elevate your thinking to a more conscious and holistic evaluation of your life. You'll begin to observe yourself and thus begin to manage your mind, actions and life decisions more attentively. Effectively, you will begin to awaken.

- **Create some space for yourself:** When you are in a dark room without windows, it is fairly difficult to see things clearly. The space you create for yourself is that crack in the wall where you allow light to come through. Leave yourself some time and space every day – perhaps first thing in the morning or half an hour before sleep, when you stay away from digital distractions and spend some time reading, writing, meditating and connecting with yourself.

- **Practice mindfulness:** Mindfulness is the key to self-awareness. Through mindfulness practice you will be more present with yourself, so that you can observe what's going on inside and around you. It's not about sitting cross-legged or suppressing your thoughts. It's about paying attention to your inner states as they arise. You can practice mindfulness at any time you want, through mindful listening, eating or walking.

- **Keep a journal:** Writing not only helps us process our thoughts but also makes us feel connected and at peace with ourselves. Writing can also create more headspace as you let your thoughts flow out onto paper. Research shows that writing down things we are grateful for, or even things we are struggling with, helps increase happiness and satisfaction. You can also use a journal to record your inner state. Try this at home: choose a half day at the weekend, pay close attention to your inner world – what you are feeling, what you are saying to yourself – and make a note of what you observe every hour. You may be surprised about what you write down!

- **Practice being a good listener:** Listening is not the same as hearing. Listening is about being present and paying attention to other people's emotions, body movement and language. It's about showing empathy and understanding without constantly evaluating or judging. When you become a good listener, you will also be better at listening to your own inner voice and become your own best friend.

- **Gain different perspectives:** Ask for feedback. Sometimes we can be too afraid to ask what others think of us: yes, sometimes the feedback may be biased, or even dishonest, but you will be able to differentiate this from genuine balanced feedback as you learn more about yourself and others. Research has shown that conducting 360-degree feedback in the workplace is a useful tool to improve managers' self-awareness. We all have blind spots, so it is helpful to get different perspectives to see a more rounded picture of ourselves.

'Accept who you are; and revel in it.'
   – Mitch Albom

I urge you to consider deeply what self-awareness means to you and factor it in to your routine. In meetings, at the school gate, when you're vacuuming – try to detach from what you're doing and observe yourself doing it. Consider whether your behaviour, thoughts and feelings align with your deeper values and your higher purpose. Reflect daily on what worked, what didn't work and what you could improve.

EXERCISE: YOUR PLEDGE

Complete the following sentence with a self-awareness practice that will work for you and note it down in your journal:

'I pledge to build self-awareness into my life by…'

BELIEFS AND VALUES

My definition of self-awareness is that it means having a consciousness of one's own values and belief systems and how they impact your behaviours.

Beliefs

The main way I transcended my self-awareness, beyond stream of consciousness journaling, was to identify and evaluate my own belief systems and values. I came to recognise the power of beliefs as either limiting or empowering, and to see how values motivated the majority of my behaviour, actions and thoughts. I also came to acknowledge the breadth of different life perspectives each individual holds as totally unique to themselves.

I can go for a winter walk in the woods and revel in the crunchy leaves, the snapping twigs beneath my feet, the view open to the sky after the leaf-fall, the majesty of the changing seasons, the freshness of the air invigorating my body and mind, exalting in nature and so on. My son could join me on this same walk and see it as muddy, cold, slippery, bleak, depressing, pointless and draining. We're both experiencing exactly the same woods, the same walk, sharing the same moment but we are perceiving it entirely differently. This difference stems from our belief systems. I believe a winter walk is a positive experience. He believes a winter walk is a negative experience. What's fascinating is that it's not just the events of our lives that shape us, but our interpretations – our self-created beliefs – of what those events mean.

So, where do these beliefs come from in the first place? As children we're all born with the same clean slate and slowly life starts to happen around us and we form our view of the world. Our beliefs are created both by our environment and by influences from carers, to teachers, to society at large. They are affected by our experiences, our circumstances, our instinctive reactions to events. Beliefs are also formed by our learned knowledge, our life research and by our past results. They become our internal representations of the world. They become the certainty we hold about the world. 'I am strong' vs 'I am weak'.

The reason I'm dwelling on beliefs here is that, in the words of Anthony Robbins, 'Beliefs are the foundation of excellence.' In his classic bestseller *Unlimited Power* he states, 'People who succeed on a major scale differ greatly in their beliefs from those who fail. What we believe to be true, what we believe is possible becomes what's true, becomes what's possible.'

So, think about a big event you've got coming up at work, a big career-changing moment, an interview or presentation. Do you believe you will absolutely own the moment and deliver your message credibly and successfully? Will this be the moment you take off and get that promotion/role/award? Or are you riddled with anxiety, nervous you will stutter, fumble, forget key content and suffer gross humiliation? Are you resolute you will fail because you always do and it's pointless even putting yourself through the cringey embarrassment of trying?

Well, Henry Ford hit the nail on the head when he said, 'Whether you think you can, or you think you can't, you're right.' It's that simple.

Ultimately our beliefs drive us towards fear or excitement. I am excited about the interview and I will succeed; I am scared about the interview and I will fail. Our natural instinct is to respond to fear by retreating and avoiding any situation that will stimulate it: 'I'm scared I'll fail at that interview so I won't go.' Do you see how any belief that elicits fear is a limiting one? If you intend to succeed in life you are going to have to face these limiting beliefs head on and knock them out of the park.

I'm not just talking about 'feeling the fear and doing it anyway'. I'm talking about exploring what's beneath the belief, pulling it apart and ultimately flipping it so it guides you towards success.

Beliefs have the power to create or destroy, to be empowering or disempowering. Just look at the power of placebo drugs: by simply believing that we're being cured our minds generate a physiological response that confirms we are indeed healing and so we do. Scientists have even documented cases of schizophrenics who change eye colour as they change personality! I had a mentee recently who told me she knows she'll be a terrible parent so she won't marry her boyfriend and start a family. She's constricting her life through a disempowering belief that may crush her relationship and, indeed, her family lineage. All because of a belief, and a limiting one at that.

The exciting bit is that you control your mind and you can choose which beliefs you want to hold on to for greatest personal gain. The way you reverse your beliefs from disempowering to empowering is by reframing them. For example, if you tell yourself when you go running that you will feel exhausted, it will be a struggle, you won't be able to breathe, and every second will feel like hell, you are unlikely to go ahead and do it. If, however, you focus (as I do) on how incredible you will feel afterwards, how your skin will glow, your body will tingle, your brain will be flooded with endorphins and you'll feel euphoric, confident and capable, you'll be in your running gear and out on the road before you know it. You can transform your mindset into focusing on the positive, the uplifting 'reframe' of the situation.

The trick with reframing is harnessing your best bits and working with your strengths. You take what energises and invigorates you the most, what drives you towards pleasure and excitement, and reframe the situation around that. Think about moments when you are in flow and look at how you can build them into your reframing. For example, I am an impatient, inexperienced and undevoted cook. I am also a spiritual person and a nutritional obsessive. I can reframe cooking as a beautiful spiritual exercise blending the benefits for body, mind and soul into one activity. I've spun cooking from being a loathsome chore I can't abide to an activity that honours my values and empowering beliefs.

'Love is what we were born with. Fear is what we learned here.'
     – Marianne Williamson

EXERCISE: FLIP YOUR LIMITING BELIEFS

What we believe totally transforms the decisions we make today (more on decisions in the 'Action' chapter) and the situations we then find ourselves in. Grab your journal and take ten minutes to write down any beliefs that are driving you towards success (your empowering beliefs), and any beliefs that are driving you away from success through fear (your limiting beliefs) and detail the projected situational impact of those beliefs, following the examples below:

Empowering belief	Situational impact
I'm a magnetising woman...	... therefore I will go out tonight, be vivacious, charismatic and beautiful, and meet the man of my dreams.

Limiting belief	Situational impact
I'm a terrible public speaker...	... so I won't accept the invitation to do the keynote at the conference.

Now spend some time reviewing your limiting beliefs and look at how you could reverse them. Take the example below of how to transform the restrictive belief of being a poor public speaker as your model.

Limiting belief	Situational impact
I'm a terrible public speaker...	... so I won't accept the invitation to do the keynote at the conference.
Empowering belief	**Situational impact**
I am a credible professional in my field and value every opportunity to share my message...	... so I will be privileged to share and enjoy communicating my message at the conference.

Next, say all of your flips out loud and put them up on sticky notes around the house, in 'Notes' on your phone or in your journal. Speak them, think them, honour them until you start to believe them and your neural pathways will create congruent positive associations.

Values

Living with integrity means respecting and honouring your values. Your values are, according to Anthony Robbins, 'the fundamental, ethical, moral and practical judgements we make about what's important, what really matters. Values are specific belief systems we have about what is right and wrong for our lives.' They are the main motivation behind everything you do, think and say. When we feel unhappy in life invariably it stems from being out of alignment with our values.

A top tip is to examine your values – what they are and how aligned you are with each other – before you commit to a business partnership or relationship.

I had a pivotal moment in my corporate life when I felt desperately miserable. I couldn't understand why I wasn't thriving. Management weren't happy with me and I wasn't happy with them. Then – eureka! During my nightly self-reflection I did some work on my values. As I listed my values, I realised that when I did the same exercise for the leadership team I was part of there was not one value we shared. We were totally out of sync. No wonder there was confusion and conflict on both sides. People or teams with entirely different value sets will never happily co-exist.

Values can't be compromised without pain. This was a lightbulb moment for me: I regained my power and realised there was nothing wrong with me; I was just in the wrong place with the wrong team and it was time to move to a culture better suited to my values. It was a liberating moment and I skipped into work the next day making plans to realign my path.

> 'Imagine you could do what brings you the greatest joy or deepest satisfaction: be with the people you love, use your natural talents, exploit your gifts to their fullest. That... is a picture of a person living according to what she values most.'
> – Henry Kimsey House, Karen Kimsey-House, Phillip Sandahl and Laura Whitworth

---

EXERCISE: IDENTIFY YOUR VALUES

Thinking about the times you have been happiest, most fulfilled and most purposeful, grab your journal and write down your top ten life values. Don't overthink it, just free flow, with no prioritisation. Anything that pops into your mind is good. (See the appendix for a list of example values if you need inspiration, but note that this exercise should be intuitive.)

Now star the top five values you identify as your priority values, those which are most important if you are to live a happy and fulfilled life. Are you currently living in congruence with these five? If not, what needs to change?

When you are living in total harmony with your top five values, what is it that are you doing? How are you contributing to the world? What is driving you each day?

Commit to making decisions in life that honour your priority values.

TRUST YOUR INTUITION

Much of the advice out there in the exploding array of self-help literature encourages us to follow our hearts, to listen to the deep inner voice showing us our true paths and ideal relationships.

If we're to follow our guiding intuition, how can we distinguish between a deep calling and wishful thinking? How do we recognise a gut-inspired path and ignore an ego-driven pursuit? When we are still and reflective, which voice should we listen to?

Reassuringly, there are ways to distinguishing the ego's voice from your heartfelt intuition. This is how to tell them apart:

1. The ego shouts and stimulates extreme sensations in the body: high-energy excitement and anticipation, or bone-shaking fear and anxiety. Repetitive thoughts, loop cycles, that 'wired brain getting stuck' state – these make you feel a sense of mental chaos. Intuition, on the other hand, is subtle and calm. It's a still, deep, gentle knowing. Whether you like what your intuition is telling you or not, there's no crazy physical or mental reaction. The knowing is almost soothing.

2. The ego is driven by logic, rationalisations, impulsive desires and an intense focus on what the outcome will give you. It is driven by gain, by an end result that feeds your self-esteem, your public image, your extrinsic world. It is without humility. Conversely, intuition is your heart, your gut. It's a broad direction without articulation of a specific, explicit goal. It's a pathway rather than an end point. You may visualise the success of a particular goal but without obsessive attachment to that outcome.

3. Your ego is driven by fear, whereas your intuition is positive internal guidance. The ego is trying to protect you from harm via a primeval

'fight-or-flight' instinct: do this to save yourself, to protect your reputation, look better and so on. Intuition seeks peace and takes you to a place where your needs are met positively for your growth.

4. Your ego can be destructive, as it's self-serving. It's short term and potentially self-sabotaging. Intuition, on the other hand, feels deliciously natural to follow and trust. You don't need an inner dialogue back and forth to justify the course it's guiding you on, you know deeply in your soul that it is right.

If we haven't been following our intuition, it may rise up to confront us as a mid-life crisis. Then we either retreat into depressed, grumbling acceptance or start making radical, often dramatic changes, to areas of our lives. Gentle changes could include more time devoted to self-care, or perhaps shunning diets, habits – and perhaps even people – that do not bring you joy.

Listen carefully to your heart. The gentle, intuitive wisdom within you is leading you to your most exceptional experiences and your highest potential. Things are pretty sparkly up there, so go and reach for those stars.

> *'Joy is what happens to us when we allow ourselves to recognize how good things really are.'*
> – Marianne Williamson

CHAPTER THREE: **Cleanse**

Energy
Self-Awareness

Action
Play
Enrichment

*'If you're on the right track doing what serves your
soul, then you're going to feel good, relaxed, and
peaceful. Your heart will beat steadily, your energy
will remain high, and you'll be relatively free from
aches, pains, anxiety, or stress.'*
– Sonia Choquette

I sat in the boardroom gazing out across the London
skyline and awaiting my managers. St Paul's Cathedral
glinted in the distance. It was an out-of-cycle meeting,
subject: 'X client', no agenda. After a few minutes
of convivial chit-chat I noticed the CEO's body language change as his back straightened, his shoulders
pushed back. The MD moved physically closer to him.
The energy in the room changed – it crackled. They
launched. Accusatory verbiage, unsubstantiated crit-
icisms, spiel overlaying an unspoken hidden agenda.
There was no invitation to discuss the topic. It was a

one-way diatribe. It hit me as an assault, unexpected and unjustified. I left the room upset and cross, frustrated at being rendered mute. The lack of collaboration, of productive exploratory discussion, these behaviours were in direct conflict with my leadership values. So, how to manage this momentary disempowerment? Either effect positive change or cleanse…

By now you have a clear understanding of who you are, what energy resources you have available to you and of the incredible power of your own mind.

This chapter will focus on a necessary part of any transformation: cleansing. When we cleanse we are ridding ourselves of that which is superfluous. When we cleanse our faces in the evening we wipe away the makeup, the dirt, the day. So it is with life. A cleansing process removes that which no longer serves us and leaves us with a neutral, clean slate ready to take into our new worlds.

RENEWING

Jeff Bezos, Amazon founder and 'world architect', has a refreshing and clearly phenomenally effective outlook. He never accepts the status quo. He relentlessly pursues better. Innovation, quick decisions and long-term thinking underpin every decision he makes. In business this translates into service, technology and eye-watering increases in share value. The bit I admire most that is relevant here is a cultural philosophy embedded into the Amazon way of working. In a public shareholder letter published in 1997 (and republished and referred to in every annual shareholder letter since – what a man of conviction and substance!), Bezos refers to Day 1 companies versus Day 2 companies.

The Day 1 companies are those that are at the beginning of their potential, with Day 2 companies representing stasis, followed by irrelevance, then 'excruciating, painful decline... Staying in Day 1 requires you to experiment patiently, accept failures, plant seeds, protect saplings, and double down when you see customer delight... In Day 2, you stop looking at outcomes and just make sure you're doing the process right. It's not that rare to hear a junior leader defend a bad outcome with something like, "Well, we followed the process".' Those companies that fail to embrace key trends quickly enough, risk being pushed into Day 2.

This means making what Bezos calls high-velocity decisions. 'That doesn't mean sacrificing quality in favour of speed, but it does mean making most decisions with only about 70% of the information you wish you had. You need to be good at quickly recognising and correcting bad decisions. If you're good at course correcting, being wrong may be less costly than you think,' Bezos states.

I love this. It gives us a little glimpse into how one of the world's most transformational leaders embraces perpetual improvement. He cleanses daily. And so should you: adopt the mindset that every day is your Day 1 by regularly taking stock, cleansing and renewing.

EXERCISE: STATE OF THE NATION

We're going to do a little bit of clutter-busting here. Let's evaluate key areas in your life and whether they need a spring clean or an almighty shunt around.

Grab your journal and draw a table like the one following, or print it off my website www.biancabest .com, populating it with the different aspects of your life to consider when you're cleansing. Put a tick in the relevant column against 'draining' or 'invigorating'. Identify actions you could take that could shift each element from draining into invigorating or enhance its invigorating power even further. I've started it off with some sample assessments and actions to inspire you. Now complete the table according to your own personal reflections.

Element	Draining	Invigorating	Action
Who			
Family			
Friends		✔	Make more time to meet up with friends
Colleagues			
...			
What			
News	✔		Only keep up with as much news as is needed to be well-informed in my area

Element	Draining	Invigorating	Action
Social media			
Devices			
...			
Where			
Home			
Work			
Holiday			
...			
Emotional			
Love			
Guilt			
Stress			
...			

SHED WHAT DRAINS YOU

In working through that exercise, you may find some patterns have surfaced that link one person/thing/ behaviour across all the categories. If this is the case it will be easy for you to zone in on that particular area and decide whether you want it in your life.

Don't get me wrong – I'm not about to ask you to immediately bin any person, thing or behaviour that makes
you feel less than gleeful, but I will emphasise that you
should avoid the brutal self-betrayal of compromise.
Of course, there's gentle give and take in relationships,
where loving respect encourages you to give a little of
yourself so your partner can receive more. As Caroline
Myss, author and human consciousness scientist, says
of intimate partnerships, 'A compromise is done will-
ingly and out of love.' So, yes get the grey paint instead
of blue if it makes your loved one that happy. But
when it comes to the big stuff in life – your work, your
home, your family, your epic decisions – don't ever
compromise your values, ignore your intuitive desires
or squash your personal perspectives. If you censor
yourself, supressing something that matters to you,
you will find it surfaces later as sadness, resentment or
anger, because you have created imbalance elsewhere.

Now, today, this minute, this second, presents you
with a moment to acknowledge what is bringing you
down and to address it.

There are five priority areas to think about when con-
sidering your own toxic elimination. These have arisen
as the most prevalent areas both for me and for the
hundreds of women I have coached and mentored over
the years, privately and within the corporate realm.

Social media and news

We exist in an era of unprecedented stimulation. Ninety per cent of the data in the world today has been created in the last two years alone. The average Westerner is exposed to 5,000 ads per day and receives an *average* of 85 notifications on their mobile device per day. And we're still speeding up. It's no wonder our senses are feeling overwhelmed. Brands, retailers, businesses, news channels, social media – it's all ping, ping, beep, beep, flash, flash, as we're assailed with endless attention-grabbers.

The impact on the human brain of perpetual digital assault is a tendency to become passive as we wait for the next notification, the next stimulus, to provoke action. We're losing the ability to think proactively, to filter and focus. Concentrated attention remains the surest route to quality output, as Daniel Goleman explores in his prescriptive bestseller, *Focus: The Hidden Driver of Excellence*, where he asserts that focus is key for human, organisational and planetary flourishing. We simply can't excel at anything without deep focus. It's just plain fact.

So how do we combat the endless stimulus and become more selective in what we consume? It's easy once you stop being a passenger on this digital roller-coaster and take back control.

Most of our consumption today happens through our devices and screens. In the marketing industry an entire science has emerged examining how to effectively target consumers through multiple screens simultaneously – TV, desktop, laptop, tablet, mobile and so on. Who doesn't gaze at their phone last thing at night before sleep, then first thing on waking up in the morning? Futurists predict that screen technology will evolve further still, with holograms and augmented reality headsets enabling anywhere to become a screen. Car windows are already being used as screens in the latest models gliding off the factory line. Screens are all pervasive and we need to manage how we digest what's on them.

With our devices, there's a simple fix: turn off the notifications. That is one easy shift you can make that immediately halts your dopamine-inducing addiction to 'Ooh another Instagram like!' Go into 'Settings' and just turn them off. You don't need to read every message as it comes in. Wait until you're ready to access messages and then digest them en masse.

Make the first hour of every day free from digital invasion. Use this sacred time to direct your thoughts and attention where they will be most useful. As described in 'CEO of the Brain' at www.theleadersbrain.org, the most productive time for our brains is just after waking, as this is when the prefrontal cortex is most active. In this fresh state we're better at focusing attention, creative writing and effective learning. This is why successful CEOs work from home for the first few hours of the day. Be a CEO yourself, make the most of those excellent brain waves while they're bounding around energetically, plan your day, do the important stuff and focus. I make a point of not looking at my phone until I am about to leave for my train, at which point I've followed my morning routine and am now clear on my day's priorities, spiritually enlivened and in a positive and uncluttered mental state. I then absorb the downloads and let the layers of stimulus build, knowing my foundations are set and strong already.

My morning routine

- I switch off the phone alarm without looking at any other display on the phone. I climb out of bed and stretch, facing out across my garden, noticing nature, as I emerge from sleep to wakefulness.

- I then down one full pint of water, standing, shoulders back (this really seems to help wake me up); I breathe really slowly and deeply as I drink.

- I immediately shower or exercise and allow the new day's thoughts to surface before I let any media consumption pollute my mind. Every single day there will be one if not several exciting, stimulating thoughts that hit me.

- I tune in to my intuition and write these thoughts down, capturing up to five actions/ideas/ perspectives/priorities before they float away. I then have a clear 'proactive' focus for my day and know what I will have achieved, progressed or explored by bedtime.

- Next there is my indulgent but wonderfully effective ritual while I apply my makeup. I used to always listen to the BBC Radio 4 *Today* programme but realised I was cluttering my brain with market fluctuations, war, terrorism, political bickering and wasting that fresh brain state we are all blessed with first thing. So two years ago I started listening to audio books instead. My audio book of choice may be a novel, or a favourite spiritual book, or perhaps a business book teaching a leadership skill. I follow my intuition and allow a carefully selected voice and subject matter to permeate my consciousness while I prepare for the day.

- Before I leave for my train I take a photo of my thought list and head on out to let the day unfold.

Social media can be as harmful as it is entertaining. Get context before you weep into your pillow at night, lamenting your lack of life success compared with those Insta beauties who are young, fit, drunk yet bright-eyed, have immaculate homes yet work full time, whose kids are adorable despite being raised by staff, etc. Get perspective, and if shiny social media perfection upsets you, well, don't look at it. Take conscious control of the social apps you consume, use and allow on your phone.

One lady I coach needs an app on her phone to restrict access to her social media channels to certain points in the day. She recognises the extremely detrimental impact her social media obsession is having on her life. It limits her productivity as she wastes hours idling on her phone looking at 'nonsense', as she puts it.

The key is to identify how you're using social media and whether that usage is serving you well. If it inspires you, connects you to your community or brings out your best self in some way, fantastic. If not, and you recognise that it is limiting your life contribution in some way, then modify your engagement with it. And ensure you're guiding your children accordingly, too.

Comedian, author and activist Russell Brand talks openly about his Instagram addiction being as chronic as his sex, drink and drug dependencies. His view is that any obsessive behaviour that is destructive to yourself or others is dangerous and symptomatic of deep-rooted psychological issues. His personal tried and tested solution to curing addiction, as he eruditely describes in his book *Recovery: Freedom from our Addictions*, is to follow the AA's twelve-step programme of acceptance, amendment and new behaviour, and to draw strength from a higher power.

I highly recommend you read it if you're concerned about your own addictive tendencies. Fundamentally, be very aware of how social media is serving you, positively or negatively.

People

According to Timothy Ferriss, you're the average of the five people you spend most of your time with, 'so do not underestimate the effects of your pessimistic, unambitious, or disorganized friends. If someone isn't making you stronger, they're making you weaker.' Let's suppose you're designing your dream life (which you now are), aiming to function as your absolute best self: wouldn't you surround yourself by invigorating, supportive, loving people who will enrich your world? People who will elicit your best thoughts, behaviours and perspectives? People who expand your mind and help you learn and grow every day?

In the workplace you will thrive when you are surrounded by peers and leaders who inspire you and teach you things you want to excel at. You'll be more engaged with your work and the corporation itself. You'll be reliable and productive, as this scenario satisfies the innate desire to learn and grow which we all hold as human beings. Who in your world inspires you, at work and in life generally? How close are they to you? How accessible? Who do you want to learn from?

My favourite Carl Jung quote is, 'The meeting of two personalities is like the contact of two chemical substances: if there is any reaction both are transformed.'

It's so true that sometimes you meet people and are magnetically drawn to their energy, their vibe, their wit, knowledge, and demeanour. Conversely, others you can take or leave; you don't feel any kind of fizz. With the magnetically attractive ones you feel lifted, energised, positive, abundant with creativity, possibility and ideas. You laugh more, you feel alive, you feel joy. Not only do you feel transformed, but when you're together life feels transformable!

In my research, observations and personal pursuit of new work, passions, friends and tribes over the years I have come to recognise the value of investing energy in seeking out those souls who will lift me higher. Yes, enhancing our potential starts within, with self-awareness, self-acceptance and self-love, but, oh, the excitement and effervescence of being with someone you connect with, someone who stimulates you to be an ever-better version of yourself. Now that is a real wow.

So why on earth would we waste one precious second on people who drain us? Why do we 'carry' friends, family and colleagues and try to ignore our weary feeling of being brought down by those around us? Generally, this stems from a sense of loyalty. If loyalty is one of our personal values, it would be too much of a conflict with our own integrity to walk away from a dispiriting relationship.

For your own growth and happiness in life, though, you need to avoid, or at least reduce your contact with, those who steal your time, energy and love. Remember, 'Energy flows where your attention goes', so be aware if it's dribbling down the drain wastefully.

The exercise you need to do now is to identify if and how you are being held back by any life zappers in your immediate environment.

EXERCISE: ZAPPER IDENTIFICATION

If you answer yes to any of the following questions, please think carefully about whether there is any merit in maintaining the relationship, and about how to set some protective parameters around it if it must continue.

- Is the relationship one-sided, in that you give, give, give and feel the other person takes, takes, takes, rarely giving anything back?

- When you think of being with this person, do you feel immediately drained and 'shoulder-droopy'?

- Do you come away from conversations together feeling exhausted (and often in need of a large white wine!)?

- Do they seem to enjoy being locked in their 'circles of suffering', enjoying the act of complaining almost more than the problem itself?

- Are they so self-absorbed that they never ask you about yourself or your life?

- Do they talk at you rather than to you?

- Do you get the impression they never listen to you? Does your advice fall on deaf ears? (Despite copious recommendations to help solve their problems, they never take heed and instead enjoy being stuck.)

- Do they love gossiping about others and share private tales you know are breaches of confidence? (If they're doing this about others you can be sure they'll be doing it about you too at some point.)

- Do you rarely laugh together? This is critical as even the toughest relationship can survive as long as there are decent bouts of shared humour.

If your friend has scored five or more yesses, you should evaluate whether you need them in your life, and consider how to detach from them if the answer is definitely not. If you must maintain the relationship, because of family or work obligations, for instance, design a mini management plan.

Zapper management plan

Expectation awareness: Don't forget that time spent with a zapper will be focused on them. Ensure you don't have any false assumptions that you'll be able to share your latest problem, story, or adventure. Go with a listening mindset, then you won't come away disappointed.

Time limit: Set limits on the duration and frequency of rendezvous. I have certain people in my life whom I love and respect, but I know time spent with them will be an exercise in tolerance for me no matter how compassionate and selfless I'm feeling. To manage this, I minimise the number of social engagements with them and when I call I state that I only have x minutes before I need to attend a meeting/school collection/etc.

Communication plan: If you know a phone call with a zapper will be thirty minutes of their download before they even ask how you are – if indeed they get to this at all – how about using text instead? Keep the exchanges as frequent as appropriate. This method of communication allows you to maintain contact and say the right things succinctly while also sharing your news.

Your tribes

It's a primordial instinct to be part of a tribe. We want to belong, to feel love, a sense of connection and a common purpose. It's wonderful when we're in sync with our gang and all moving in the same direction.

Each one of us has multiple tribes of varying prominence contributing to our sense of wellbeing. For my teenage daughter these tribes are her school pals and online social community. For my mother it's our family, unequivocally. We're the only group that matters: she relishes our bond and doesn't feel the need for a wider social life –who needs friends when you have family? For me and probably for you, I have my familial tribe, my friend tribe, my work tribe, and I'm now creating my wellbeing tribe (insert your own passion/hobby/ interest group). Each one brings a different sense of belonging and connection, reciprocal support and meaning to the daily grind.

It's never been so hard to belong to communities of any substance and longevity. Gone are the Victorian days of the street community. Gone are the days of the job for life. Gone is the solidity of love partnerships till death do us part. There's volatility and flux everywhere. Deep down this messes with our heads, hearts and souls.

Along with our choice of which community to join or grow comes the choice of which tribes to reject. Flip it round, and you have the dreaded outcast scenario – when you are rejected by your tribe. When your company decides your contribution isn't what the organisation needs. When your husband leaves you for a younger model. When the 'in crowd' want you out. When you just can't break into an industry circle you believe you should be part of. Rejection is rife, an inevitable part of life and, yes, it hurts.

So how to cope with tribal rejection? How to make sense of the destabilising closed door?

Our instinct is to satisfy the primitive needs of belonging and to cling desperately and rather pathetically to the group/person/tribe we've attached ourselves to. We become rather shallow versions of ourselves, flailing around trying to prove that we are still quite fabulous and they are lucky to have us in their gang. The corporate outcast scenario is particularly painful to witness. The extra graft, the over-delivery, the perpetual feedback requests: 'Am I doing okay? What did you think of that?' – all vapid because in our cut-throat workplaces once you're out, you're out.

Don't demean yourself by wasting effort on a tribe which is consciously shunning you. No, take heed. Get the picture; get with the painful programme. Open your eyes wide and move on.

It does undermine your confidence so comprehensively you wonder how you'll ever stop the tears from flowing and pick yourself up again, but, my dear resilient, beautiful friend, you will. If that tribe doesn't want or need you and your gifts, there will undoubtedly be an even better, warmer, more richly engaging tribe just around the corner waiting for your positive and passionate self to join them. Your responsibility now is to detach emotionally, see the situation for what it is, and move positively towards the brighter horizon.

When you're feeling knocked back, rejected and at odds with your tribe, step back, accept that that tribe was just one chapter in your life journey – a fleeting moment that has served a purpose and now gone. It's time for a fresh community where you'll flourish, and life will be back to being played on your terms. Never, ever forget life is a choice and choosing who you hang with is essential for living life with joy. Go find 'em and move on up!

Romantic partnership

This is a biggie and one we cannot ignore, as your life partner is probably your most significant other, the missing piece of you, the wind beneath your wings, your soulmate. Or is this all trite nonsense, and your life partner is there for money, sex, good times and shared parenting? Perhaps they are there for a depth of connection, with shared visions and values that make your life journey all the more exhilarating and joyful?

Only you know where your romantic partnership ranks in your life prioritisation, but we cannot neglect this huge area of life and I want you to take an honest look at this relationship. Does it need work to elevate it to its truest potential or should you be bidding each other farewell?

EXERCISE: A TRIBE OF TWO

Grab your journal and complete the following statements about your love partnership:

- The values we share unequivocally are....
- The version of myself I become when I am with my partner is....
- We laugh together over...
- Our happiest times are when we...
- Our saddest times are when we...
- Growing old together for us looks like...
- When I think about our relationship I feel...

Commitment

If you're focusing on non-essential tasks and frittering time away on moments that are unrelated to your higher purpose and long-term goals, why on earth are you wasting your precious energy on it? It's all very well aspiring to run the PTA for the third consecutive year, but only if it aligns with your soul's ultimate calling (which presumably in this instance is unburdening other stressed parents, fastidious organisation in the service of others, and a bit of glory seeking!).

In my gap year between A-levels and my degree, I moved out of home and worked full time in a publishing company. I was on a mission to get work experience and a salary, and to savour independent London life. I loved flicking through my Filofax (yes, I'm that old!) and seeing a full week of evenings spent with other people. I would tingle with satisfaction to know it was Priya on Monday, Jo on Tuesday, team drinks on Wednesday, college friends on Thursday, clubbing on Friday and so on. An empty evening slot made me wince.

My ego was insecure and screaming, 'Be with someone!' The sad thing is that these people weren't necessarily forever friends. Often these were new, random pals who seemed as up for fun as me, aka as lost as me. Whatever drove me to behave this way (fear of loneliness, desire to look popular, making up for the lack of a boyfriend?) I eventually realised empty white wine evenings with strings of acquaintances were not the way to a fulfilled and happy life (not to mention the bank balance depletion caused by bimbling from one Soho wine bar to the next, night after weekday night).

We need to take a careful look at what it is we are spending our time on, how are we filling these precious, ever-diminishing hours of our lives and why.

These searching questions will help you to consider how wisely you are spending your time:

- What is your most valuable contribution to life? If your strength is networking and rapport-building then go ahead and fill your diary with engagements, like I did. But if you're devoted to teaching energetic balance and harmony, then practice what you preach. If you're a writer, why erode your cognitive function by drinking alcohol to the point of inhibiting your creative flair? Respect the talents you have and honour the value of your contribution every day.

- Are you behaving in a purpose-driven way? Are you honouring your big fat Why (more on this in the 'Action' chapter)? When you conscientiously pursue your goals – be they short or long term – it's easy to direct time and energy into the right areas. Consider your behaviour in all realms of your life and check in on what is or isn't leading you towards your ultimate life purpose.

- Is whatever you are doing aligned with your values? When you dishonour your value system you will not find congruence between what you do and what you feel. If you are working with a team who don't share your values you will be in conflict and unhappy. If they respect autocracy, hierarchy and aggression while you respect kindness, humility and acceptance, there will never be harmony. Cleanse anything that prevents you from honouring your personal values.

- Check in with your intuition. If you're with someone, or somewhere, or doing something that leaves you feeling mentally exhausted and physically sagging, you need to move on. Trust your subconscious: when you follow it wholeheartedly it will always lead you to your highest excitement.

- Get comfortable saying no. Far too many women grow up as people pleasers and give away their power. Don't let this be you. Enjoy asserting a confident decision that you can own absolutely. Never agree to do something that doesn't sit right with your heart or which is non-essential. When your boss delegates their dirty work – for example, handing over line management responsibility for an underperforming team member, tasking you to deliver the performance management news (as happened to me once) – step up and express your views on how the situation should best be managed, and don't simply say yes based on hierarchy. In fact, you'll actually gain more respect from your managers when you do present an intelligent alternative perspective.

EXERCISE: SEVEN-DAY DAY YES/NO CHALLENGE

Give yourself a seven-day challenge to review every commitment request that comes your way. Every time you have a moment where you can answer yes or no, pause, breathe, think and reflect. Ask yourself whether you want to commit to this, logically and emotionally? Explore any misalignment and see if you could find a route to making yes work for you, or calmly explain why your answer is no.

At the end of each day reflect in your journal on how many times you said yes or no, and how empowered or not you felt after having given your responses. This exercise will alert you to how easily we slip into doing things unconsciously, floating down the stream of life. You're not going to do that any more: you are going to choose which direction you swim in.

'You have to decide what your highest priorities are and have the courage – pleasantly, smilingly, non-apologetically, to say "no" to other things. And the way you do that is by having a bigger "yes" burning inside. The enemy of the "best" is often the "good."'
– Stephen Covey

Sometimes in life you have to honour a commitment that doesn't tick every personal box for you but you can't avoid it. Rest assured that there are ways to reframe these moments so you can indeed take back control. I once had a period when I felt incredibly disempowered in a corporate role – remember how I began this chapter. I was blocked at every turn and going into the office felt like a battle. I felt miserable and trapped for weeks… until I flipped the situation. Yes, I had to work to pay the bills; yes, I had tried every route to change the internal status quo; yes, I was fervently job hunting, but ultimately, I couldn't escape the working environment I was in for that little while. So I flipped it. I sprinkled my sparkle dust onto the situation to get the power back into my own hands and determinedly eliminated my negativity and disempowerment. How did I do it? I walked into that office every day knowing that my absolute highest contribution and biggest joy in life is to help others. So, amid the toil and the politics I embraced each day with the thought, 'Who can I help today?' I would then go about my business supporting, training, mentoring, coaching and helping anyone who needed me. I was spreading my knowledge, nurturing and kindness. Of course, I did the work I was being paid to do, but I made sure my day was packed full of purpose-driven fulfilment by squeezing in as many moments of enlightening others as I was able to.

I quickly regained a clear sense of who I was and felt cleansed. I became energised by being in the office again – energised by my interactions. The more I was authentically me, honouring my values and intuition, and saying no whenever professionally appropriate, the stronger and brighter I grew, and before I knew it the hands of fate had propelled me back on to my happy path. Doors opened rapidly, leading me to an exciting, shiny new chapter in my career. I flew onward and upward away from that business, grateful for the learning experience, and with proof of the truth of the universal law that 'doing what you love brings you more of what you love'.

Time management

One of the keys to having it all without cracking is effective time management. Defined by www.mindtools .com as: 'The process of organising and planning how to divide your time between specific activities. Good time management enables you to work smarter – not harder – so that you get more done in less time, even when time is tight and pressures are high.' It's that last bit that's so exciting. When you manage your time brilliantly you actually get more done but without burning yourself out. When you focus on the right things at the right time in the right order you achieve the right results – those glistening results you so want. But time management itself takes effort and commitment. Once you do it well, however, life becomes a breeze.

As my life filled with more work, more play, more homes, more children, more businesses, and more commitments I realised I was spinning a lot of plates – an entire school dining room's worth of plates. I was queen spinner and the only way I could successfully spin them all was through fastidious time management. So, after taking inspiration from Steven Covey and one of his famed seven habits: 'Put first things first' (taken from the bible *7 Habits of Highly Effective People* – please read it; I can't recommend it enough), I took to differentiating the urgent from the non-urgent and the important from the non-important. I basically prioritised in a careful, ultra-selective manner, and then I hosted a family meeting and prioritised for them, too.

Every Sunday afternoon would see me plotting out the next week in full. What do I intend to achieve next week? Where do I need to go? When will I exercise? Which kid is doing what where when? I would plan out my personal and professional appointments for the week, even going as far as diarising when I'd go for my runs or workouts, and which parent was doing which school run on which days. It was all organised into my schedule so I didn't have to panic about squeezing these things in as the week unfolded. I had created the time I needed to do what I wanted to do and so the week would then flow. Of course, there were always curve balls and inevitably urgent work would steal time or a child would be sick, but for the main part my weeks rolled out as planned.

As soon as you get into the routine of managing your time this way it becomes effortless, and as you involve the family in this process it becomes fun, too. There's a lot to be said for the children being part of an adult discussion once a week around what it actually takes to run a busy household. Why shield your children from the effort that life takes? Teach them early on to respect the benefits of planning and structuring family time around one another.

I'm not saying diarise every single waking hour, as it's essential to have delicious blocks of empty time for play and spontaneous activities (more on that in the 'Play' chapter later), but I am emphasising how much more time you *create* when you organise yourself to focus on what matters most.

If you don't prioritise your time, others will prioritise it for you. As Greg McKeown teaches in *Essentialism: The Disciplined Pursuit of Less*, 'Essentialism is not about how to get more things done; it's about how to get the right things done.' I'm proud to be more productive than ever, and to have more impact on the world than I've ever had in my forty plus years on this planet; all while sleeping more, exercising more and having more family time, all thanks to time management, so I encourage you to follow suit.

I've recently started enjoying a flurry of compelling invitations to conferences, dinners, speaking engagements, meetings and more. My universe has expanded into one of abundant opportunities and fascinating people. I'm invigorated and have enjoyed saying 'yes, yes, yes', as I *want* to do everything. But… I recognise that even when motivated by both a logical and emotional desire to say yes, I still need to manage my time carefully. There isn't enough time in life for everything; nor do I have unlimited stamina to do everything, however alluring it may be. I am a limited resource and must be mindful of that. My current manager inspired me with the provocation to say no to every fifth invitation. I'm employing this rigidly now and am extremely conscious of how I filter my yesses.

Physical detoxification

It would be remiss to have a chapter on cleansing that didn't cover detoxifying your body. Basically, to detox is to cleanse the blood. There are numerous detox diets and treatments around, from juice fasts to sugar cleanses, colonic irrigation and dry skin brushing. Fundamentally they all work to eliminate the toxins stored inside you by resetting your system to aid efficient bodily cleansing. I discussed the role of the liver earlier, in the 'Energy' chapter, so you're well aware of how important the liver is.

Any internal cleanse will focus on ensuring the liver is performing as it should. Otherwise harmful toxins, both those formed inside the body and from external sources, are not eliminated and remain in our system, leading to a strained immune system, which can trigger inflammation, allergies, sensitivities and infections. The liver is also involved in the elimination of hormones, blood sugar balance, the production of bile, and storing nutrients, so a healthy liver is vital to our overall health.

Any external cleanse will focus on opening skin pores to release toxins through our body's largest organ – yes, that's our skin. From dramatic Indian yogic-inspired retreats to saunas to a Turkish hammam body scrape, there are multiple options to activate elimination.

You can choose to detox your diet sporadically, by going on a restrictive diet every few months, for instance, or you can do twelve-hour intermittent fasting every night if that works for you. Investigate what appeals to you, always trusting your intuition to guide you towards your best option and always respecting your bio-individuality.

When I cleansed my diet radically for six months in August 2017, eliminating alcohol, sugar, gluten, wheat, dairy and caffeine, I felt so amazing I have tried to avoid or limit these items as permanently as I can sustain. After only a few weeks following my new way of eating I had lost pounds, I was glowing – and I mean luminous – with radiance, and I felt reborn. I was almost skipping instead of walking. I was so energised I was buzzing. And oh, the clarity of thought! I felt mentally razor-sharp. And, yes, I've slipped back into drinking champagne and eating chocolate now and then, and, ooh, I love a good cake, but for the main part I know living toxin-free results in my happiest, most productive and unequivocally best self. So I advise you to experiment with what works for you, identify your own pollutants (for example, dairy may not impact you in the same way that it affects me), and once you decide to detox, set your timeframe, plan your schedule around it and don't waver in your commitment. Do it properly and you'll love the results.

Purifying the mind

Mindfulness, meditation and spiritual practice of some form are other good ways to cleanse mentally – see the relaxation section in the 'Energy' chapter. Again, do your research and trust in what appeals to you most. I was privileged to take part in a no-speaking retreat in a Thai Buddhist monastery, which was a fabulous introduction to Vipassana meditation: moment-to-moment awareness was the intensive focus for fourteen consecutive days. I carry the training from that period with me daily and step back into mindfulness as often as possible. It helps slow life down and I always feel that I gain time somehow after moments of conscious awareness.

A good tip is to use the shower as a daily moment for connecting deeply inside your body. As the water flows down over you, take deep, slow breaths and become totally aware of the water droplets falling onto your skin; become present in the richness of the moment. When you breathe deeply it also stimulates lymphatic drainage, so just by breathing you can be cleansing. Easy!

Moments of presence are where you achieve peace and thus purity of mind. Eckhart Tolle's *The Power of Now* remains my favourite Audible download for a reminder of the uplifting gift of presence.

> '*Whatever the present moment contains, accept it as if you had chosen it.*'
> – Eckhart Tolle

Cleansing is just one part of your journey to radiant energy and I'm sure you'll find more fabulous ways to cleanse that work for you. Good luck and please join our www.yourlifehack.com community for more advice and support on moving on.

CHAPTER FOUR: **Action**

'Everything can be taken from a man but one thing;
the last of the human freedoms – to choose one's
attitude in any given set of circumstances, to choose
one's own way.'
– Victor Frankl

With an exaggerated flourish I perfected the organza ribbon adorning the silver gift wrap. I deliberately savoured the process, finessing its shape, the stiff wire creating a perfect, retail display-worthy bow. I felt serene despite the late hour, soothed in the knowledge this would be the last parcel I would ship after a decade devoted to my personalised gift empire. This was the end of an era. The last nocturnal manufacturing effort. The final furlong.

I had decided to sell my business after market conditions and my personal circumstances had changed.

It was a positive decision. The company had served me, my customers, my staff and my family well. Acknowledging that this chapter was concluding was not hard. In fact, it was liberating, empowering, exciting. Once I had made the decision to sell, my ambition took on a new thrust. I felt expansive again. My energy levels increased as I prepared to find a buyer and to explore a fresh tomorrow. This wasn't a door slamming; it was a kind farewell, a gentle transition with the glimmer of something twinkling on the new horizon. As I looked towards an unknown future I was spurred into thrilling, bountiful action. My ideas flowed, my to-do list expanded exponentially, my eyes opened to endless opportunities, I came to life again. I was animated by the limitless potential of a new career direction. Action was utterly invigorating...

Now we're getting down to the nitty-gritty. We're moving beyond the soul-searching and inner work into tangible, life-shifting commitment to build on the previous three steps. Well done you for all your work on self-discovery. You now understand your Productivity Balance System and your energy flows, and have your own process for enhancing self-awareness. You've identified your values and started flipping your limiting beliefs. You've cleansed your life of food, things and people that don't serve you, and are ready to move positively into a state of action. Effectively, you're now going to bring all of your deep thinking together, get organised and build your personal strategy for success.

I've opened this chapter with a Victor Frankl quote as it powerfully emphasises the gift you hold in being able to determine your destiny. He suffered horrendous atrocities and survived where others didn't through dogged strength of mind. He chose to focus positively, never wavering in a hope born from unbreakable belief in his greater purpose to work as a psychotherapist outside the concentration camp. In his deep exploration, *Man's Search for Meaning,* Frankl teaches us that once you understand that attitude is a conscious choice, once you harness the power of your mind and understand how to direct it, you can remove limitations and withstand whatever conditions or circumstances you find yourself in. Maya Angelou similarly tells us, 'If you don't like something, change it. If you can't change it, change your attitude.'

When we examine change it's important to understand that the psychology behind it is such that we are only motivated to step into the challenge of activating transformation when the pain of staying where we are is greater than the anticipated pain of the transition. Think of every strong woman who steps into divorce aware that she will cause disruption – to her children's stability, to the sanctity of the marriage, to living arrangements, to social groups, never mind the financial disputes, the risk of personal battle and so on. But she remains driven by the certainty that emerging out on the other side of the separation will be better than the ache of staying. It's not a case of the grass being greener over there, but of the existing grass being muddy, debris-ridden and stagnant. The desire to be released from the suffering today, to achieve the better state, is greater than the fear of the impending transition. It's what I call the 'motivation equation'.

FINDING YOUR PURPOSE

There's much chatter today around higher purposes being the key to happiness. 'Follow your passions and your dreams will materialise' and all that. It's all quite vague, though, isn't it? When you're working your daily grind, ploughing through your to-do list, you may whimsically dream that building a school in Africa or saving the whales is your higher purpose but it's too far removed from reality. 'In another lifetime' I hear people say, 'I'd be a… ' – fill in your blank.

Let's just clarify what I mean by your purpose. I'm not talking here about a role, a thing, an outcome, but more about your calling, your passion, the thing that makes you zing. There are few people in the world who recognise from adolescence how they will make their mark on the world. Most of us struggled enough with puberty and social integration as we carved out an independent existence away from parents or primary caregivers, never mind following a heartfelt passion. We fell into careers rather than pursuing them purposefully. We then dutifully progressed up the career ladder until one day we opened our eyes and wondered why we were doing what we were doing and how we got there, and so the classic mid-life crisis hits. The earlier you can connect with your true purpose and passions in life, the quicker your path to happiness.

I've always been proud to call my CV a chronology of passions explored. I didn't know at eighteen that my life purpose would be to empower others to step into their best selves, but I always knew I found joy in writing and communicating to inspire, motivate, and build energy and connection. These activities have so far fuelled the roles I've held and the businesses I've created. As I write, I feel hugely excited by leveraging the platform of my corporate leadership role today to simultaneously create flourishing work cultures. I feel blessed, invigorated and 100% aligned with my life purpose.

Let me help you identify yours.

EXERCISE: LIFE PURPOSE

Thinking about the earlier exercises on empowering beliefs and values, I'd like you to consider your 'life purpose': a higher goal that is a manifestation of what living these values and empowering belief systems means to you.

You might want to begin by asking yourself that question. Or you might change the language to refine this concept for yourself. You could also create a mind map to understand your purpose, beginning in the middle with the words 'my reason for living is…'

Noting your responses in your journal, start by trying to express your purpose in two words, if possible: a verb and a noun. You might find then that the full sentence flows more easily. Some examples might be:

- Inspiring beauty
- Supporting women
- Challenging thoughts
- Creating value
- Valuing time
- Living passionately
- Building frameworks

You will know once you have your purpose as it will just feel right. Tell some trusted friends and colleagues your purpose and see what their response is. Once you get this clarity of purpose everyone, including you, will see how perfectly it fits. You now have your North Star, your guiding force, your direction.

Now that you have your purpose, it's time to move on to the next phase: crafting your mission statement.

'The only difference between people who are truly abundant and thriving spiritually, emotionally, romantically, financially, and professionally and those who are stuck, stagnated, and feeling they are missing out and living the same boring, depressed, and small life is that those who are truly abundant know their Purposes and are living them daily.'
– Mastin Kipp

EXERCISE: MISSION STATEMENT

Take a look at some of the mission statements of the following people – of whom no one could say that they hadn't found their purpose in life!

- Sir Richard Branson, founder of the Virgin Group: 'To have fun in [my] journey through life and learn from [my] mistakes.'

- Amanda Steinberg, founder of Dailyworth.com: 'To use my gifts of intelligence, charisma, and serial optimism to cultivate the self-worth and net worth of women around the world.'

- Oprah Winfrey, founder of OWN, the Oprah Winfrey Network: 'To be a teacher. And to be known for inspiring my students to be more than they thought they could be.'

Have a go at writing your own mission statement in your journal.

Remember values and mission statements change across the course of our lives, so it's important to reappraise regularly. Experts teach us that to remain relevant and motivating it's essential to update your mission statement as you evolve along your journey.

My own life purpose is: 'To empower ambitious individuals to step into their best selves.'

My mission statement is: 'To epitomise kind, effective leadership by harnessing my vibrancy and acumen to inspire others to make their greatest impact.'

INTENTIONALITY

You've now articulated your purpose and written your mission statement. You have clarity on your ultimate intention in life. Now let's explore what living with intentionality entails. Let me tell you now that it's liberating, motivating and utterly compelling. It makes life easier to navigate on so many levels. But note, any life goals you set, decisions you make or actions you take should be in congruence with your mission statement. Misalignment here will mean trouble later on.

When you embrace intentional living, every day is fuelled with drive and pace, and you will shift into an empowered, productive state. You will have a direction, a sense of destiny. The focus you now apply will transform multiple aspects of your life.

When I was thirty-three and found out I was pregnant with twins, I decided to have the babies at home in water. This was unheard of in the UK at the time, apparently making me the first woman in the South East of England to birth twins at home for fifty years. I had to present my case to a board of regional midwives and sign indemnities that I was responsible if, heaven forbid, anything went wrong. Everyone asked, 'Are you sure, are you really sure?' But I never once faltered in my knowledge that having them at home was the right thing to do. I trusted my body and my intuition. The decision was easy.

Being resolute, I took complete responsibility for that decision by ensuring my body, mind and soul were absolutely ready to deliver those babies happily and healthily at home in water. I focused on meditative rituals and positive concentration daily for nine months and, sure enough, I gave birth at thirty-nine weeks in a birthing pool at home to two beautiful, miraculous baby boys. The habits that I had introduced were self-hypnosis, optimal nutrition, gentle exercise, visualisation, avoiding negative media/people, etc. I took total control of owning my goal, honouring my decision and setting myself up for success.

It worked and I'm blessed to count the experience of delivering my first twin Sebastian all by myself as the midwives, my mother and my husband watched on, in the warm water, under the soft dim glow of my lounge chandelier, as one of the most exquisite, empowering, beautiful, 'women-rule-the-world, I-am-capable-of-*anything*, love-is-explosive' moments I have ever lived through. The alignment of body, mind, nature, the universe, destiny, stars, rainbows, God, whatever – it was all synchronised in one spectacular, glorious event. For that I am truly grateful, and I don't think it was just good luck that meant I wasn't in hospital having a C-section at thirty-four weeks. I had the birth I planned.

When people say I'm lucky to have my home, family, career, energy, etc, I say I've created my own luck. None of this has happened by chance. I have focused, worked, and intentionally created all that I have and will continue to do so. Living with intentionality is indeed empowering, but there's a responsibility that comes with desiring and then achieving a life of balance and success. It will never be handed to you on a plate. You need to commit consciously to creating the life you desire.

I never put a wish out into the universe then sit back and wait for it to be fulfilled. I recognise the remarkable effect of marginal gains and the satisfying feeling of inching closer and closer towards each dream every day. I construct habits that align with my goals and enable me to achieve them. I reflect daily on whether the habits are working, whether I am making progress, whether my decisions have empowered me. If so, great! I'll continue. If not, I'll call a halt and change strategy. Ultimately, I respect the power of the decisions I make.

DECISIONS

The energy released when you make a decision to step towards your goal or vision is incredibly invigorating. According to Howard Thurman, 'In the wake of the decision, yes, even as a part of the decision itself, energy is released. The act of decision sweeps all before it, and the life of the individual maybe changed forever.'

Similarly, Anthony Robbins teaches us that 'It's in our moments of decision that our destiny is shaped.' So, respect and understand the power of your decisions. Every extra chocolate digestive you eat, every pint in the pub, every moment of procrastination, every time you bury your head in the sand, everything you do shapes your future. Do you really want that body or lifestyle or home? What tomorrow do you seek?

Whatever your decisions, make them consciously and commit to them.

I've found when I've entered periods of sobriety, I've always been excited by my decision. A dry January, a sober October, or a whole six months off alcohol – these always fill me with brain-tingling excitement about what lies ahead. I don't feel restricted or hard done by; on the contrary I exalt in my decision, in its authority, and immerse myself totally in it. I get giddy with the power of having decided to give up booze.

As I write I'm on a flight to Las Vegas for a global technology conference, where I have an eye-watering schedule of meetings, seminars and exhibition tours, plus once-in-a-lifetime invitations to champagne cocktail receptions in chandelier-adorned bars, club nights with celebrities and so on. I'm even more excited than usual as I've decided to experience the next seven days totally sober. I want to be fully present and not dull a single brain cell for one second. Perhaps this doesn't sound like a big deal, but once I'm in sequins and in a glamorous setting I'm usually the first to quaff the Veuve, dahling! So this is a considered, conscious decision.

I debate endlessly with a relative over abstinence from alcohol, as she is forever lamenting, 'Oh, I shouldn't drink any more, but I so want to; oh, it's so hard not being able to treat myself,' and so on. She's in a perpetual state of non-commitment to her decision to give up. It's unrelenting martyrdom. She oscillates between 'should' and 'want' and never finds peace in either drinking or abstinence – well, she's happy enough when she's tipsy and dancing in the rain! She has failed wholly to embrace her decision, which thwarts her progress in sticking to it, bless her.

Ultimately, ask yourself if you want to be a passenger or pilot in life. Are you continually being swept up by the current, passively and reactively being dragged along against your will? Or do you consciously take control and swim in the direction you want to go? Think back over your words, thoughts and actions: it won't be hard to spot the disparity between woolly decisions that you haven't implemented and committing to a defined direction.

EXERCISE: THE COMMITMENTS

Here are some simple steps for committing to your decisions. You can use your journal to note down your thoughts and plans.

1. Organise your thoughts and write down each decision

2. Elaborate on the specifics of why, what and how

3. Scenario-plan for moments of weakness and think about how you will stick to your decision

4. Prioritise and organise your life to honour each decision

VISION SETTING

'In order to carry a positive action we must develop here a positive vision.'
– Dalai Lama

My life is a manifestation of my visions. Are you familiar with Rhonda Byrne's bestselling book, series, and film *The Secret*? Have you heard of the 80s Abraham Hicks duo and listened to some of their law of attraction seminars? Is it baloney... or is it fact? Well, for about ten years I had a picture by my bed of a beautiful mansion, with an orangery, overlooking spectacular grounds. Last year, as our kitchen extension was finished, I had a flash of realisation that I had manifested my vision. It had happened – and not by chance. I had determinedly worked towards achieving this dream my whole life. Hard graft and focus yield results, and knowing what you're aiming for stimulates intensity of action. So I believe wholeheartedly in the merit of vision setting.

For their thirteenth birthdays, I give each of my children and godchildren a personalised keepsake box emblazoned with '[Name of child]'s Dream Box' on the lid. I encourage them to store in it pictures and things they want to have as part of their future, be it perfume bottles, magazine images, flowers, jewellery – anything that piques their interest as a desirable part of their idyllic life. I encourage them to get collecting from a young age, and to focus on these dreams with vibrant clarity, so that their reveries feel a little more tangible and real.

I still have a diary from when I was sixteen that has a magazine image I'd stuck on the front showing a glamorous olive-skinned brunette business woman in a gorgeous white trouser suit smiling vivaciously and obviously rocking her work world. I have moments when I catch myself in the mirror and it's that cut-out smiling back at me. (I'm not quite as youthful, don't have as abundant locks, nor that Hollywood smile, but I'm a happy, slim, fit, positive working woman in a similar suit with that olive skin!) The things we imagine from a young age set us on the path of aspiration. So, start your kids consolidating their dreams early. It really does focus the mind. As Carl Jung said, 'Only the dreamer knows the dream.' It's yours to own.

So let's start having some fun. We're going to create a vision board.

EXERCISE: VISION BOARD

- Discern your intentions
- Gather your supplies
- Create space
- Find your images and words
- Paste them to the page
- Put your vision board somewhere that you can see it
- Write a 'make it real' list
- Notice and address any resistance

Now live your vision daily. The process of neuro-responsive association means that with enough emotional intensity and repetition, our nervous systems experience something as real, even if it hasn't happened yet, so

- Write your mission statement out and stick it everywhere
- Make your vision board prominent
- State your intentions out loud
- Journal and reflect on your progress
- Keep adding to your dream box/vision board/ journal descriptions
- Meditate on your vision daily

GOAL SETTING

You must have crystal clarity on your goals. Only once they are defined can you design strategies to reach them. Start by establishing your short- and long-term goals, then plot the habits you'll need to introduce for your exceptional life to materialise, where all of these goals have been achieved – and achieved with gusto. Think about your morning routines, your daily, weekly and monthly habits.

First, let's explore three ways to ensure your goals are explicit, and personal enough to motivate you at the deepest level. Then we'll move on to some science and practical steps for introducing habits.

Goal setting 1: SMART goals

When it comes to goal setting, ambiguity simply won't work. You may be familiar with 'SMART' goal setting from the professional world. Goals are:

- Specific
- Measurable
- Action-oriented
- Realistic
- Time-bound

This model is often used to create personal development plans defining clear aims to help you contribute effectively to your team's agenda and specify your personal work objectives. The opposite of a SMART goal would be a broad-brush-stroke goal of, for instance, being 'a high-performing team'. This is a meaningless goal until you specify exactly what success looks like. How much revenue denotes high performing? Earned within what time frame? And exactly what deliverables equate to high performance?

Businesses become far more accountable, productive and equipped to achieve when they have SMART goals. This approach can be equally powerful in your personal life where you set out each aspect of what you hope to achieve in detail. Here's how I might apply them to my fitness regime, for instance:

- **Specific – What exactly do I intend to achieve?**

  A six-month commitment to achieving peak physical fitness. My workout will comprise a high-intensity training plan comprising 5k on the treadmill, and abs, back and arm exercises.

- **Measurable – How will I measure success?**

  I will have a personal trainer (PT) assessment before and after. My resting heart rate will lower, I will feel more energised, be slimmer, my body mass index will improve and I will be able to run faster for longer.

- **Action – What precisely will I do to achieve this goal?**

  I will do this workout at least five times a week, at 6.30am every work day before my commute. I will go for five-mile uphill runs with my dog whenever weekend schedules and weather permit. I will book the PT assessment.

- **Real – How realistic is this goal?**

  This is completely do-able, providing I am not at a work function late the night before, or ill.

- **Time-bound – When will I complete this goal by?**

  I will complete this goal in six months from the first of next month.

Simply saying 'I want to be fit' just wouldn't be detailed enough. If I don't define it to the nth degree, the goal is too loose. Would the generic goal of 'being fit' mean running once per week or daily? My brain wouldn't be able to grasp the goal fully, or be able to commit to it fully, and in fact I'd be wasting time and energy on muddled thinking ('Well I did run once last week but I don't feel fit…'). The exact goal needs specificity.

This is where the SMART goal methodology is fabulously powerful. It organises our thoughts into details which in turn are more likely to lead to success. Be disciplined with this tool and to ensure congruence use it when working through the additional two models of goal setting described here.

Goal setting 2: Goals with soul

Now I invite you to consider your goals through the lens of how you want to feel. What's your desired *emotion*? Danielle LaPorte, an American life coach and inspirational speaker, highlights the benefits of creating 'goals with soul' in her book *The Desire Map*. She encourages us to ensure all our life goals become meaningful by tying them to emotions we hope to feel. She asks us to look at different areas of our lives to identify which emotions we are most drawn to and then for these desired feelings to become intentions. If you examine what you are doing now, or have been doing, and divert your attention from the behaviour and shift to focus instead on the resulting emotion, what do you see? How do you *feel* about having done what you have done, or doing what you do? Do you need to change things to feel differently, indeed, to feel better?

Here are some sample word associations that could elevate your goals into the realm of the soulful, the emotional. Play around with different areas of your own life and brainstorm inspiring words for every aspect of your life.

Aspects of life	Inspirational words
Health	Luminous, vibrant, vital
Relationships	Passionate, connected, loving
Work	Fulfilling, enriching, stimulating
Money	Liberating, abundant
Spirituality	Enlightened, alive, calm

It's a bit of fun, and definitely adds a deeper dimension to your goal setting – the spirited bit. For the fitness goal example, I'm going with 'alive, powerful, present, vibrant, grounded'. See how it lifts the goal into a more motivating one?

Goal setting 3: Know your Why

When I ask my daughter to tidy her bedroom she grumbles, fusses and resists, and the end result is less than acceptable. When, however, she asks to go to a party and I agree on the proviso that she cleans her bedroom, well, we enter a whole new world of focused effort. She will spruce that room until it's catalogue-worthy and offer to do the twins' bedroom, the hallway and the whole downstairs too. When she has a strong why, my goodness it spurs a whole different level of input.

Neuroscientists tell us that 80% of success in anything is down to psychology and only 20% mechanics. Deep mental engagement is more powerful than physical actions. It's why one athlete, with the same equipment, techniques and course, will outperform another: it's their mental conditioning. Simon Sinek, in *Start with Why*, describes how the power of connecting with your why builds more emotional intensity around your goal and ultimately drives success. 'Working hard for something we don't care about is called stress. Working hard for something we love is called passion.'

Last year, my son Sebastian lost his ability to back-flip on the trampoline. One day he could, the next he couldn't. He'd done a flip that went slightly awry, landed at an awkward angle, hurt his neck and was scared of repetition. His fear thwarted his ability to perform, or even attempt, a backflip again for a whole year. It took a great deal of mental conditioning and coaching to finally coerce him to feel confident and proficient at backflips again. Only once his why for mastering the skill again – envy at his twin brother's trampolining prowess – became omnipresent, could he squash the fear holding him back and get reverse airborne again.

Nietzsche, the German philosopher and pioneer of the Enlightenment, famously stated, 'He who has a why to live can bear almost any how.' Fundamentally, when we know why we do something we're more driven to do it. Let's go back to my fitness goal: why do I want to be fit this year? Well, I want to be the best mother I can be and to perform at my highest level at work, and I know being fit will improve my brain power, compassion and energy levels. That's far more motivating than just 'wanting to be fit'. So think seriously about your why(s) as you work through your various life goals.

EXERCISE: GOAL SETTING

Okay, now it's time to bring these three models together and design your own goals. Use the template below and complete it three times: for the short term (three months), mid-term (six months) and long term (twelve months and over), across each of your main life aspects, for example, health, work, relationships, money, spirituality. Of course you can add/delete/edit life categories according to what is relevant to you. Design your goals in line with the three techniques I've described above: SMART, 'goals with soul' and finding your why. Be ambitious, be real and be focused – take your time with this exercise. Once these goals are on paper, you've decided you're committing to them, and remember how transformational taking ownership of your decisions is. Grab your journal – and get specific.

Life aspect: 3/6/12+ months	SMART	How will achieving this goal feel?	Why do I want to achieve this?
Health			
Work			
Relationships			
Money			
Spirituality			

THE POWER OF HABIT

Fantastic, well done! You've now established your goals for the short, mid and long term. This is huge progress. How do you feel about these goals? Different from the previous occasions you've set life goals? I sincerely hope you feel more deeply connected to everything you've plotted out and excited about what it will be like once you've hit them all. Our next step is to become 'habit architects'. We're going to build or adapt all the catapulting habits you need to get you where you want to go.

I'm a huge believer in habits being integral to your success. My personal experience has shown me that effectively and deliberately managing my habits, culling those that harm me while building in positive habits, has the power to up-level my life stratospherically. From curing insomnia by addressing my coffee and sleeping tablet habit, to creating daily spiritual routines, to Sunday night family scheduling, and so on, addressing my habits has released me from my old burnout cycles.

Look at the Oscar-winning actor Bradley Cooper, who attributes every bit of his success to obliterating his bad habits, namely pharmaceutical drugs and alcohol. In a *New York Times* interview described by Groth, he stated, 'I was doing these movies… and I'm sober, and I'm like, "Oh I'm actually myself. And I don't have to put on this air to be somebody else, and this person still wants to work with me?" … I was rediscovering myself… and it was wonderful.'

Equally, when we look at the most successful business leaders, inventors, thinkers and technologists – the people who have shaped and are shaping our worlds for the better, there's a consensus approach to habits:

1. **Their habits align with their goals, giving behavioural congruence and clarity on where they are going**

   High performers are clear about what they are doing and how it relates to their best future selves. They are fastidious about progress rather than perfection and live by the rule of marginal gains: small steps leading eventually, not immediately, to big leaps. As described in an article by Nick Ward, the cyclist Dave Brailsford applied this with dramatic effect to Britain's Team Sky, creating an unprecedented, winning formula: 'The whole principle of marginal gains came from the idea that if you broke down everything that could impact on cycling performance… and then you improved every little thing by 1%, when you clump it all together, you're going to get quite a significant increase in performance.' And so it is for each of us individually. It's a case of knowing your purpose, designing goals to reach that future destination, then enjoying the step-by-incremental-step pathway to your best future self.

2. **Intentionality**

High achievers resist the drift. They live by the mantra 'Autopilot is the enemy of intentionality', being clear and purposeful not just about their actions and their behaviour, but about what they expect from their efforts and interactions. Designing a tight habit rhythm obliges you to slow down and make conscious, deliberate choices.

3. **Setting and keeping standards**

All high achievers have high standards. If you, or your team (if we're in the corporate realm) accept substandard performance and no one is held accountable, then poor performance becomes the new standard. What you preach doesn't matter; it's what you tolerate that counts. How can you drive excellence as the new average?

4. **Making impact and outcome their obsession**

The most successful leaders share a relentless focus on results and outcomes. They keep on trying to be more productive, more impactful, and always have their eyes on the end goal – think of Elon Musk at his Tesla factory, where he invites every single employee to suggest ways to improve the business. Perpetual innovation and refining the status quo to improve tomorrow is intrinsic to success. How could you refine your habits to stimulate better results?

PRACTICE WHAT YOU WANT TO GROW

The beauty of habits is that the more you undertake a task the stronger your neural pathways become. Brain scans prove that the more we do something, the more pathways in the brain we create; over time these strengthen, bulk and expand, until we've quite literally built a new area of the brain capable of delivering that task. The more repeatedly you act, the more neurons you grow, making the act more and more unconscious until it happens without cognitive strain, which frees up your brain power to do more new and exciting things. Remember what we learned about unconscious competence in the 'Energy' chapter? That's what this is. Create the habits, and practice what you want to grow and you will form the unconscious competence. It's not magic, it's science, and completely within our grasp. Shauna Shapiro, neuroscientist and brain surgeon, delivers an inspiring TED talk titled *The Power of Mindfulness: What You Practice Grows Stronger*. She describes how the neuroplasticity of repeated experiences changes the brain: 'We can actually sculpt and strengthen our synaptic connections based on repeated practice.'

I've realised that over the years my habit of running several times a week has become total normality for me. I don't have to waste any brain power persuading myself to go, I'm in an automatic zone where I identify myself as a runner. I look forward to time alone listening to my books, enjoying nature or the intensity of the treadmill high, the amazing way my body feels, the company of my dog running alongside me, the positive emotions the motion itself produces and so on. I've effectively tricked my brain into seeing running as an integral part of me – and I really don't think it took that long to become a pleasant, positive habit. I hope this encourages you to believe that any habit you desire can be yours for the taking.

Charles Duhigg, author of *The Power of Habit*, identifies what he calls the Habit Formation Loop, a cycle made up of reward systems and cues which stimulate habit creation. He teaches that certain cues trigger certain behaviour, which then gives us a certain emotional reward. So, if you want to break bad habits, you will need to become aware of your trigger moments, modify your behaviour and yet still gain the same emotional reward. To give you an example, I battled for years to give up coffee. Despite reading about willpower, mental control, and publicly blogging about my intention to quit, I failed time and time again – until I used Duhigg's method. I examined all the moments I would weaken and realised that I associated coffee as a treat or a pick-me-up. If I'd had a great meeting I'd pop into Starbucks for a latte; if I'd had a terrible night's sleep with a sick child I'd treat myself to a warm, frothy cappuccino. This would happen repeatedly, despite me writing down every loathsome personal association I have with coffee: it was a poison; it was wrecking my sleeping patterns, making me jittery and jumpy at work, etc. I'd write the 'Cons to Coffee' on my notepads, mirrors, car dashboard, yet still I perpetually caved in at these trigger moments of 'deserving to reward' myself with a feel-good brew.

As Duhigg advised, I had to break the routine. I had to design a new habit in response to the cue that would deliver the same reward. So, after a successful meeting, my celebratory, milky drink was replaced by a phone call to my mother. (Admittedly, she freaked the first few times: 'Oh no, Bianca what's happened?' she gushed in shocked panic at a call in the middle of the working day.) When I had a long day lay ahead I replaced a caffeine-laced pick-me-up after zero sleep with a hardcore ginger juice punch – way more invigorating and flooding my system with goodness. I achieved the same, satisfying emotional reward each time, but without the toxin in my body. I'm relieved now to have been caffeine-free for years.

EXERCISE: YOUR TRANSFORMATIONAL HABITS

It's time now for you to examine your habits and direct them towards exceptional living, as your best, most productive and fully intentional self. Think about your morning routines, your daily, weekly and monthly habits; collate everything you've learned and the decisions you've taken as part of each exercise you've completed in your journal so far. It's time to identify the habits you want to introduce into your life to help you deliver against those goals and attain that higher purpose which is unique to you.

Choose one goal for each of your life aspects and consider which habits you will need to change or introduce to move you towards that goal over the next twelve months.

Consider cues which will trigger either a positive or a

negative habit and become aware of the feeling the reward generates.

The following questions will help you draw up a plan for replacing old habits and/or introducing new ones.

- What cues will you need to become aware of for both positive and negative habits?
- What rewards will reinforce the habit?
- What will committing to the habit involve and feel like?
- Why should you commit to the habit regularly?
- When will you begin?
- Grab your journal and use the template below to help you plan your change of regime.

Life aspect	Habit to change/ introduce	Why	When	Cues	Rewards	Commit-ment	Feel-ing
Health							
Relation-ships							
Work							
Money							
Spirituality							

CONSCIOUSLY COMMIT

Now you've committed these habits to paper it's up to you to take full ownership of delivering against them. Be proud, focused, excited and positive, and remember it only takes three weeks of repeated action for a habit to form (some scientists claim it can happen even sooner).

Ultimately, when you take mental control of a situation and apply the right attention any life change you desire is possible.

Top tips:

- Don't play the victim
- Don't be swept downstream
- Respect the power of your decisions
- Choose your attitude
- Consciously plan to achieve

Before we conclude this Action chapter, a few words of advice on balance through the lens of success. It's exciting to get carried away with wanting to change the world, by designing endless goals, introducing multiple tantalising habits, launching out into invigorating action, but do pause and remember that overdoing it leads to burnout. Be selective in what you prioritise; focus on what you're good at and what energises you; delegate or delete the rest. Consciously factor relaxation and breathing time into your new habits. Remember that on our deathbeds, we don't reflect back on the work that we did but the depth of connections we formed, the loving and the giving that enriched us, our lives and the lives of our loved ones. Prioritising a drive towards success defined by money and power is not the route to a life of fulfilment. Never compromise your wellbeing, relationships or inner happiness in pursuit of these things. Instead, take the time to clarify what success truthfully, personally means to you. It is ultimately in your power to halt your whirlwind and obliterate the modern-day plight of time famine. *You* can create the time you desire.

Energy
Self-Awareness
Cleanse
Action

CHAPTER FIVE: **Play**

Enrichment

'Necessity may be the mother of invention, but play is certainly the father.'
     – Roger von Oech

We gently meandered through the cemetery, the buggy wheels purring and rattling against the melodic birdsong. Ashley babbled happily, absorbing the bountiful distractions of scampering squirrels, pecking magpies and falling blossom. I had done this walk a thousand times. A shortcut from home to the high street. As my toddler excitedly pointed out the wildlife I observed the graveyard anew. I noticed strewn crystal gemstones glistening atop graves. I saw the wiry bristles of the squirrel's tail magnified. I noticed artful spiderwebs adorning holly leaves for the first time. I clocked dewdrops decorating petals and was suddenly awed at the intensity of the pink blooms abundant in the spring trees. Through the eyes of a child witnessing the world with innocent wonder, I too was suddenly awash with fresh clarity and renewed gratitude at the privilege of Nature's abundance...

In *The Five People you Meet in Heaven*, Mitch Albom tells the poignant tale of the death of eighty-six-year-old Eddie, a fairground engineer, and his revelatory journey into heaven as he 'awakens' and understands the meaning and consequences of his life through deep introspection: 'This is the greatest gift God can give you; to understand what happened in your life. To have it explained. It is the peace you have been searching for.' As Eddie rises up into the candyfloss pink divine realms (Albom writes my most treasured phrase in the book: 'serenity without solace is meaningless') he experiences the youthful physical strength and buoyancy he's been bereft of for many years. He is light and playful, free of pain and muscular restriction. He runs along the ethereal boardwalk of his life, arms outstretched as though hoping to fly – a typical carefree child's stance. Albom reminds us that 'the running boy is in every man, no matter how old he gets'.

And that's the point here, as we explore play. Playfulness is an innate part of us. Creativity never dies. It's our natural state, no matter how old we get. Sadly, life and its endless events, influences, interactions, interpretations, beliefs, and so on, crushes our instinct to follow fun/joy/play/creativity as we leave our childhoods. From senior school onwards, we're segregated into 'creative' right brainers or 'rational' left brainers. By adulthood we're confirmed in our belief that we're either creative or not.

Only now are psychologists highlighting the necessary congruence between our left and right brain functions. Only once we fully embrace both left and right, yin and yang, shadow and light, creativity and logic, and fully connect these polarities do we reach a state of optimal flow and life fulfilment. When we learn to love the beautiful blends of energised and calm, excited and still, that we represent and abandon guilt and self-criticism, we can start to step into new levels of joy and to experience life with new vibrancy, in glorious Technicolor.

So now, in the penultimate step of our six Energy-SCAPE™ steps, let's find a way to unleash your playful and wonder-filled self back into the world. We'll start with an exercise inviting you to reconnect with your inner child, with that time when pursuing joy was your number one, unfettered purpose in life, then I'll share some of my own experiences and stimuli for this process of rediscovery. Enjoy this next exercise as a reflective, indulgent – and hopefully happy – exploration. Ideally, grab a photo or several photos of when you were a child, at any age up to ten years old, moments captured when you were visibly happy and carefree.

Please note, though, if you had a traumatic or unhappy childhood, this is not an appropriate exercise for you; your heart will tell you instantly, and you must listen to it. Skip the exercise and move straight on to my recommendations for play.

EXERCISE: YOU, THEN AND NOW

Cast your mind back to when you were an exuberant child. Picture a day/moment/place where you were happy, curious, exploratory, hedonistic, joyful... Take a moment to breathe all of that in and meditate on it deeply. It could be one moment, or it could be several. Really take yourself back and remember every feeling, every smell, sound, sensation, impulse. Now describe in your journal who you just rediscovered, using the headings below.

- Key characteristics
- Dominant emotions
- Passions
- Desires
- Key people
- Happiness triggers
- Unhappiness triggers

Next, picture yourself today, yesterday, last week and last month, focusing on certain moments of joy and pleasure or otherwise to describe who you generally are today.

Compare your responses then and now. Can you spot the recurring elements that have always fed your passions? Sum them up by completing the following sentences:

- What energises me most is...
- What makes me happiest is...
- The people I like being with are...

Make sure you capture any other observations.

And now let's translate these into a pledge along the lines of:

'I will introduce play into my life by doing [activity] every day, [activity] every week, [activity] every month, and [activity] every year.'

How did completing this exercise feel? Most of my clients shed tears throughout this session. Why tears? As those innocent, joyful emotions surface, there's often a sadness that arrives simultaneously. That sadness stems from an acknowledgement that life is now far from being as carefree as it was in childhood. Now our lives are filled with stresses, stressors and responsibilities that have trapped us into behaving sensibly (for the good of my family, my career, etc, we rationalise). This perceived burden sadly often sees us eradicating the natural joy in our hearts and turning our backs on frivolity and play. This is remiss, however, as it's fun, frivolity, play and creativity that are so enriching for our souls.

When I work through this exercise, I remember a picnic with my mother and sister and our two dogs. I feel warm July sunshine, I see infinite yellow buttercups and I feel total, utter, ecstatic bliss. I'm exalting in being outdoors, wild, free, mucky, messy, chasing the dogs, cuddling, laughing. I am free of baggage, I have no stresses/strains/fears/anxieties. I recall a serene and beautiful sense of togetherness, safety, security and overflowing love.

I feel incredibly blessed to retrieve this memory and it teaches me that I feel happiest, most energised, most creative and playful when I'm surrounded by my loved ones and by nature's glory. So this is exactly what I build into my life – our recent puppy purchase has been the most important, most defiant move to make sure that at least twice per weekend, come rain or shine, the whole family goes out for a walk together. It's fun for everyone!

What did *you* discover that you can now seize hold of to build more of that inner child joy into your world?

PLAY WITHOUT SELF-DESTRUCTION

All too often, as we enter adulthood, we shift into leisure activities that centre on drinking and late nights. This becomes our new play. For me, having children was a wake-up call and I needed a return to frivolity that didn't involve self-destructive drinking and late-night clubbing. Learning to see the world through my children's eyes and joining in their innocent play became such a joy I embraced it all as much as they did. I felt that the time I spent totally devoted to playing, whether in the woods or doing a puzzle or just reading stories, was totally rejuvenating; these moments of joy were truly invigorating. I would feel my heart expand, my body become centred, and the world seemed suddenly full of limitless possibilities. Creative play brought me back to life, especially after a tough day in the corporate world juggling politics, egos and endless challenges.

And so I started to revere creativity. It became a source of personal therapy for me. When I set up my first business, The Bespoke Gift Company, the hours of writing personalised poems for customers and designing photo montages were inspired, stimulating days of boundless fun and potential. The more creative I became, the more accomplished and happy I became.

Now, back in a corporate role running an emerging technology division, I build creativity into my life by writing my blogs, creating Instagram shots, vlogging and designing project websites. I recognise how important it is to keep creativity in my world. I also run outside for pure pleasure and delight in home renovations – I'm always planning the next room revamp or colourful flowerbed. I work an element of play into every single day and I know from personal experience how much it enhances my productivity and the positive impact I have in my world.

'At work play has been found to speed up learning, enhance productivity and increase job satisfaction; and at home, playing together, like going to a movie or a concert, can enhance bonding and communication,' according to Lynn Barnett, Professor of Recreation, Sports and Tourism at the University of Illinois. 'Playful adults have the ability to transform everyday situations, even stressful ones, into something entertaining.' Barnett co-authored a study that found that highly playful young adults – those who rated themselves high on personality characteristics such as being spontaneous or energetic, or open to 'clowning around' – reported less stress in their lives and possessed better coping skills. Perhaps they have these attributes because they are better able to keep stress in perspective. According to Barnett, 'Highly playful adults feel the same stressors as anyone else, but they appear to experience and react to them differently, allowing stressors to roll off more easily than those who are less playful.'

How we play is as individual to each of us as a fingerprint. From building with Lego, which is how David Beckham said he likes to control stress, to David Cameron decompressing at the end of a long day with the video game *Angry Birds*, to stamp collecting, to climbing a mountain, it's not what we play but the fact that we do that is so important. Play is part of our primeval make-up. Psychiatrist Stuart Brown, founder of the National Institute for Play, in California, states: 'What all play has in common is that it offers a sense of engagement and pleasure, takes the player out of a sense of time and place, and the experience of doing it is more important than the outcome.' He goes on to explain that play is a basic human need as vital to our wellbeing as sleep, and that when we don't play enough, our minds and bodies notice. We may become cranky, rigid, feel stuck in a rut or feel victimised by life. As Brown explains, 'To benefit most from the rejuvenating benefits of play we need to incorporate it into our everyday lives, not just wait for that two-week vacation every year.'

YOU ARE A CREATIVE SOUL

We are all creative. Every single one of us is creative. You are creative. I'd like to dispel the myth that only artists are creative and to stop you thinking in rigid polarities of either/or, that is, either creatively or logically minded. There are so many different types of creativity, from the quirky 'acting-of-out-of-the box' decision, to making conversation, to expressing ourselves through the clothes we wear and the hobbies we enjoy.

The impact of creativity on our souls is growing in popularity as therapy for mind disorders. Art therapy, drama therapy and dance/music therapy are being integrated with relaxation and traditional psychotherapy techniques to treat anxiety and depression – with credible success rates. *Psychology Today* finds that 'There are creative interventions that specifically focus on verbal communication and self-expression as part of treatment, such as drama therapy, creative writing and poetry therapy, and bibliotherapy. In all cases, these approaches are "brain-wise" interventions that stimulate whole-brain responses to help individuals of all ages experience reparation, recovery and wellbeing.'

The impact of creativity on our souls is vast, especially once we achieve a state of flow. Scientists have proven the neurological and psychological benefits of free-flowing creativity, that is, productivity that pours forth effortlessly, meaning you lose all track of time and are utterly engrossed in the task you're completing. This is when work becomes play (which is what I personally believe all work should feel like). Daniel Goleman, author of *Focus: The Hidden Driver of Excellence*, identifies high achievers as those who've honed their ability to focus sharply despite today's era of unstoppable distractions. They know how to achieve 'flow states'. He emphasises that those who co-opt tried and tested mental practices – mindfulness, meditation, focus preparation and recovery, positive emotions and connections – are able to gain new skills, and perform successfully, while others do not.

All this play, creativity and inducing flow isn't just about the psychological and practical positive impact on life, it also more brings us closer to Maslow's utopia of self-actualisation as it generates more spiritual joy and serenity. Essentially, play brings peace. Sonia Choquette, in *Trust Your Vibes*, teaches us to relax, play and make space for miracles to enter our worlds. She advises that when you follow your heart and 'go with the flow', your intuitive abilities increase and your ideal path – that road less travelled – becomes all the more obvious. Perhaps most wonderfully, not only are you more directional and purposeful generally in life but you're more alluring to others as when we are in the uplifting state of 'create and produce' this raises our vibrational frequencies making us more magnetic, positive and attractive, so a realm of inspiring new and/ or deeper connections opens up.

Have you closely watched your children when absorbed in their games? I observe my youngest child immersed in play, arranging his toy knights and mythical beasts, lost in his imaginary world, and I notice his serenity. His breath is slow and steady. He is un-distractible, his ideas abounding as he designs battle lines, defence zones and imaginary combat. There's a gentle joy-fulness in the sanctity of his creative concentration – despite the monsters and attacks!

Okay, let's get specific now. Here are some pointers for you to consider as part of your inner child rediscovery.

• Leisure and pleasure – what do they mean to you? In your frenetic world of juggling family and work, what does downtime currently comprise for you? Does the weekend arrive and see you carting children from clubs to parties, in between domestic blitzing, topped off with a curry/pub/night out leading to a sludgy, hungover Sunday? Do you binge-drink, escaping from the working week with 'just a few glasses' of wine with dinner that turn into a couple of bottles and spending the recovery Sunday staying in? Evaluate what the ideal definition of 'leisure and pleasure' is for you. I strongly suggest you share your ideas with the family, too, and get their input into the discussion. Design collaborative family downtime as well as finding space for your own solitary play.

• Hobbies – do you have any? With today's unrelenting schedules it's a rare woman I meet who works full time, has a young family *and* has hobbies (well, excluding the punishing workout schedules of high-achieving women who cite their 6am exercise regimes as their hobby!). If you set yourself a goal of starting a hobby, what would you choose? Hobbies don't have to be expensive, time-consuming or cumbersome. A hobby can be as simple as making soup on Saturdays. The point is to plan in something that isn't work or routine domesticity, something just for you that you enjoy. How about stargazing, camping or writing a song? Have fun!

- Consciously dispel any negative mental state with therapeutic creativity. If you're blocked for life inspiration, feeling directionless and floating aimlessly, or down/depressed/upset/angry, wallowing in melodrama, try to deliberately step out of yourself by doing something creative. Quite often the activity itself is contemplative and soothing for the brain. Even tasks generally perceived as mundane, such as clearing out a cupboard, organising your nail varnishes, chopping vegetables for a rainbow salad, or baking a cake can serve as therapeutic activities that boost your creativity, settle your neural pathways and shift your state into one of positive, focused flow.

- 'Fake it to make it' with a whopping great smile. Play with your own mind and trick those endorphins into release by smiling, smiling and smiling some more. The psychology of faking it to make it has been proven repeatedly. Smile your way into a frivolous mood and before you know it you'll be happy and infectiously upbeat. Smiles are deliciously contagious. Just watch what happens when you smile at every stranger who makes eye contact with you next time you're out. Suddenly, the world is teeming with friendly souls.

- Have fun with how you present yourself to the world. I build creativity into every single morning, delighting in the frivolity of the day's outfit, from silk to lace, boots to heels, delicate pendants to chunky bling, maxi swathes or formal crispness, demure or bold – endless options and fun! I invite you to do this too if you don't already: show up for every day like you mean it and damn well want to be there! Dress to impress in a way that invigorates you and feels like fun. Don't conform. Bring your authentic self to the fore and be uniquely you. Life feels easy when you're not trying to compromise yourself into invisibility. A chap in the office once commented to me that I looked like I was going to a wedding. I took that as a whopping compliment as I always want to dress with 'wow'. My reply? 'My God, you should see what I actually wear to weddings!' There's a renowned recruitment leader in my industry, a beautiful, strong, empowered woman, who only ever wears white. Wherever she goes she is stunning, groomed, confident and spectacular in pristine outfits. She has become legendary for it. What could you become legendary for?

- Adopt the perspective that life itself is a game. In *Playing the Matrix*, Mike Dooley brings this philosophy to life with practical guidance on working with the universe to manifest your dreams. Subscribe to his daily, free 'notes from the universe' at www.tut.com/account/ quicksignup for a chuckle. He invites us to enjoy life as an adventure, a fun game to play.

'If music be the food of love, play on.'
    – William Shakespeare

Energy
Self-Awareness
Cleanse
Action
Play

CHAPTER SIX: **Enrichment**

'Have more humility. Remember you don't know the limits of your own abilities. Successful or not, if you keep pushing beyond yourself, you will enrich your own life – and maybe even please a few strangers.'
– A L Kennedy

I stepped off the stage, surreptitiously unhooking my microphone from behind my ear. A queue of piqued delegates was quickly forming as they vied to talk to me, stimulated after my keynote. I was flooded with euphoria, gleeful and buoyant at having delivered my message in a way that had clearly stirred audience attention. The pre-performance nerves, the hours and hours of rehearsals, endlessly learning my script, the careful crafting of the visually dramatic slides – it had all been worth it. I had done it. Success! Two hours later, back in my hotel room, alone and sitting reflectively in silence, I felt an emptiness. The glory of the adulation, the emotional high that I had felt, had now faded into seeming irrelevance as my phone blinked with the usual stream of work emails, school WhatsApp notifications, training deadlines, teenagers' requests for money, the monotony of real life... on it rolled. What was the point of all of that energy, effort and gain? What was the real point to any of it?

Moments like these make me question our pursuit of endless highs. The highs we so often strive for are fleeting, temporary pinnacles of one goal achieved. The hollow low that invariably follows a high – the 'what next?' – arises when we're out of kilter with our life's purpose, when we haven't connected meaningfully with the work that we are doing, the way we are spending our time or the people we're surrounding ourselves with.

When you rise up to a state of consciousness and harness inner wisdom, veering away from extrinsic factors into internal repletion, when you become more soulful, that is when you navigate life's ups and inevitable downs without bleak deflation; that is when you redefine success on your terms. In the words of Paulo Coelho, 'What is success? It is being able to go to bed each night with your soul at peace.'

When I was a little girl my grandfather gave me an A5 postcard which I pinned to my headboard. I still treasure it today. It was a simple poem which struck a deep chord with me, even at such a young age. It has shaped my life's philosophies, my behaviours and my intense 'cherish today' attitude. It reads as follows:

Do not look back and grieve over the past, for it is gone.

Do not be troubled about the future, for it is yet to come.

Live in the present and make each moment so beautiful that it will be worth remembering.

Such precious advice, isn't it?

Now back to you. Congratulations on completing these preceding five steps. You've come on an epic journey of self-discovery and immense growth already. Next (not finally, as this is the start of an even more magnificent journey) there comes the cherry on the top. Once you've respected your energy rhythms, become fully and continually self-aware, cleansed yourself of what was draining, designed your goals, developed constructive and enjoyable habits, and built creative play into your life, there's a tantalising, glistening, 'icing-on-the-cake' way to look at your life, in which you quite simply enrich it. The idea, as in the poem, is to make each moment so beautiful that it will be worth remembering.

This chapter is structured around ten ideas to help you enrich your newly rediscovered best life through your empowered best self. They're ways I've found to add extra sparkle and sizzle to my world and I hope they will inspire you to follow suit. Please enjoy and give them a try.

STOP, RETREAT AND RENEW

> 'There is nowhere that a person can find a more peaceful and trouble-free retreat than in his own mind... So constantly give yourself this retreat, and renew yourself.'
> – Marcus Aurelius

Respect the necessity of taking a break. Whether it's family holidays where you relocate to a new location – hopefully leaving domestic drudgery behind you – to spiritual/fitness/spa/painting retreats, to leaving the office and the strip-lit boardroom and opting instead for an outdoor walking meeting, ideas and inspiration flow best when you are away from the maelstrom. Plan ways to enrich your life geographically, with refreshing new spaces and plan in the gift of time to think – or unthink!

As I write, I'm beneath a blossom tree in my garden instead of at my desk. I fancied a new location to reju-venate my creative flow and refresh my perspective (visually and mentally). As the proverb goes, 'A change is as good as a rest.'

BE KIND

'By simple mathematics giving is key to the world you seek to live in. If I take I alone gain. If I give or share then two at least are enriched.'
– Rasheed Ogunlaru

The path to rediscovering our best selves invariably starts by rediscovering how to be kind to ourselves, as you've learned throughout these pages. Be kind and thoughtful about what you put in your body, shift your thought patterns to positive, revere sleep, create time and space to allow yourself to breathe – and richness of mind will come. Obviously, one of the most effective ways to increase kindness levels holistically in your world is to reach out and proactively be kind to others. Kindness has been proven to slow aging, cure depression, improve relationships, lower the risk of heart disease and have a raft of other benefits, not least of which is the fact that it's deliciously contagious, so it spreads goodness and happiness like wildfire. The act of being kind alleviates stress and moves you out of self-centred anxiety and busyness into a positive state of giving. Kindness wafts grace and gratitude inwards and outwards, spiritually and societally. Embrace 'random acts of kindness' each day – surprise someone with unexpected kindness for which you expect no reward – and read the empirical science of Dr David Hamilton, in *Why Kindness is Good for You*, where he states that in our interconnected world, everything we do affects other things. 'This is encouraging because it means that when you are kind, you are usually affecting more than the person right in front of you... An act of kindness is like a pebble dropped.'

LEARN

'Most people are mirrors, reflecting the moods and emotions of the times; few are windows, bringing light to bear on the dark corners where troubles fester. The whole purpose of education is to turn mirrors into windows.'
– Sydney Harris

We live in a unique era, the information age, where globalisation means that thanks to technology-driven connectivity knowledge has never been so accessible – indeed, new knowledge never been generated so rapidly. Knowledge sharing increases our collective value, as we disperse new knowledge upwards and outwards, sparking new ideas. We have a plethora of sharing and learning tools available to us: YouTube, podcasts, community sharing networks, books, blogs, e-learning programmes, online universities and so on. It's possible to expand your mind limitlessly in whichever direction you choose. Lessons are everywhere, whether they're presented as such or not, and there has never been such a wealth of 'spiritual' self-help material.

So take time to consider how you learn, what you want to learn and how you can practice what you want to grow. I also recommend you find a mentor. In Thomas Friedman's bestseller *Thank You for Being Late* he states,

'Two experiences stood out from the poll of more than one million American workers, students, educators and employers: successful students had one or more teachers who were mentors and took a real interest in their aspirations, and they had an internship related to what they were learning in school.' His research found that the most engaged employees invariably ascribed their workplace success to having had a professor or professors who cared about them as an individual or who supported their goals and aspirations. Having internships in which they were able to apply what they were learning was equally important. These workers, he found, 'were twice as likely to be engaged with their work and thriving in their overall wellbeing'. So, take heed and organise yourself to identify what you believe will be most beneficial for you to learn at this moment in your life, how to learn it and who to learn it from.

LISTEN

'Seek first to understand, then to be understood.'
– Steven Covey

Learn the power of empathic listening and avoid the tendency far too many people have of listening with the intent to reply rather than the intent to understand. Shift into deep, attentive listening and always allow others to finish communicating their message. Don't pre-empt what they have to say, don't interrupt, don't respond with your own story or with an assumption; listen hard then reflect back what you've heard, and ask questions if you need clarification. It's such a simple, yet effective way to improve communication in any context, from negotiations, to leadership, to teenager management, to marriage. Practise this consciously and watch your relationships flourish.

YOUR WORK, YOUR PASSION

'This is the real secret of life – to be completely engaged with what you are doing in the here and now. And instead of calling it work, realise it is play.'
– Alan Watts

Richard Branson has always maintained that there should be no separation between work and play as it's all living. I agree wholeheartedly, which is why I proudly and happily refer to my CV as a chronology of passions explored. If I'm not personally inspired by the mission I'm working on, I struggle to maintain the energy to successfully complete it. I'm not naive and respect that for every single one of us there will invariably be work tasks we must fulfil that don't rock our worlds, but if you can reframe these as rungs on a ladder towards that larger goal, and chunk them down into bitesize, achievable jobs, you will get them done. I'm a macro thinker and admit that intricate details bore me, so I delegate this where I can, respecting the synergised impact on productivity when the micro-thinking is delivered complementarily by someone else. It means I spend the majority of my working life in a zone of energised, effective invigoration.

Have you indulged your passions in your life? Do you truly connect with the work that you do? Once you're clear about your fundamental higher purpose, your life's Why, swing into action and honour it. Work at and with your passion; make your work play. Once you achieve this you will find total congruence and fulfilment, and inner peace, with no more desperate striving for balance as your work and your life will become one beautiful continuous blend of play, of living. The British philosopher and author Alan Watts teaches us that it is 'better to have a short life that is full of what you like doing than a long life spent in a miserable way'. Touché!

CARING

'Each person leaves a legacy – a single, small piece of herself, which makes richer each individual life and the collective life of humanity as a whole.'
– John Nichols

I almost fainted recently in Stockholm. Alone on a business trip, fit, healthy, walking back to my hotel after a light supper, I suddenly felt the cobblestones beneath me rise up and sensed I was about to pass out. I fell into the closest doorway, an old-world, low-beamed café where I collapsed into a chair by the door. I didn't lose consciousness and goodness knows what caused that funny turn, but the compassion of the restauranteur was heaven sent. He was a total stranger, an Afghan working in Sweden to fund his family back home, lonely and disappointed by life's struggles, yet he nurtured me through my shaky vulnerability like a best friend, a close relative, a soulmate. It was human nature flourishing, our innate predisposition to care for others. He didn't pause for one moment before rescuing me with kindness and lemonade, and I'll be grateful for his tenderness forever.

Now here's a plea from me to you if you're a parent. If you don't already, please seize the gift of parenting for the blessing that it is and dismiss the mindset that childcare is a chore. Savour it, as it will be gone in the blink of an eye. In the words of Cinderella in the latest Disney version of the story, 'Have patience, have courage and be kind.' This is exactly what nurturing young souls requires. You are the adult and it's within your gift to perform the parenting role with steadiness, consistency and love. It is a privilege to have children seeking your help and guidance, and one not to be taken lightly.

Turn your phone off, cancel the coffee morning – be present. Get down on the floor and play with them, listen to why they're upset, tame your own anger, place them above the superfluous aspects of our busy, bustling worlds. Relish teaching and inspiring your little ones day by day, preparing them to launch themselves confidently into the world as young adults, and be proud in the knowledge that you gave your best and enjoyed every inch of the shared journey.

Caring doesn't stop at the school gate, though. Through the teenage years and onwards we'll be their guides.

The voices we hear in our heads as adults are those of our parents – chastening, advising, reminding, teaching. The wisdom you impart at every stage will linger. Of course, caring also means looking after our own parents or guardians as the generational cadences shift. Whether caring upwards or downwards, it takes utter selflessness and really gets to the heart of what matters most in life.

INSPIRING RELATIONSHIPS

'The way you get meaning into your life is to devote yourself to loving, devote yourself to your community around you, and devote yourself to creating something that gives you purpose and meaning.'
– Mitch Albom

Remember what we covered in the 'Cleanse' chapter? I described the effect of a meeting of two personalities as being akin to a chemical reaction that transforms each of you forever, and therefore the impact that others can have in shaping your average self. Never lose sight of this. Seek out those who inspire you, and drive you forward and upward. Invigorate yourself with those who make you laugh, who love you unconditionally and who you can be your raw, beautiful, unaffected self with.

I am blessed to have a rich array of loyal friends and family to lean on, learn from and treasure. One friend will inspire me to exercise differently; another to experiment by drinking no wine, only pure tequila; another with bone broth for gut microbiome health; another for uncontrollable laughter and so on. And beyond friends, my colleagues, who enlighten me with their fresh perspectives, help broaden my horizons daily. We all have dependable beings in our worlds who help us thrive, and it's important to identify who those faithful ones are, where they are and what they're doing for us to enable us to live our best lives.

My husband has gracefully stepped into doing more school runs than me, is a better cook than me and keeps the laundry flowing through our home impeccably. Without him supporting me, indeed all of us, I couldn't travel and work as I do, and certainly not without the comforting knowledge that the children are content and all is stable at home. We've worked hard and consciously to achieve a harmonious state that enables our best family dynamic to work and the fragility of each day is something neither of us take for granted. I am endlessly grateful to my husband for enabling me to flourish, and I tell him so. Who are the rocks in your world and when did you last say thank you?

JOURNALING

'Journaling is like whispering to one's self and listening at the same time.'
– Mina Murray

We addressed the power and benefit of daily writing as a spiritual practice back in the section on self-awareness, so this is simply a reminder. If you haven't already started your journaling ritual – whether long form, short form, typed, hand-scrawled, at a desk or on the train – do explore the impact of reflecting on each day of your life with a moment's journaling. In Greg McKeown's aforementioned book *Essentialism: The Disciplined Pursuit of Less* (which I gifted to my entire agency leadership team to stem the 'endless over-whelm and non-essential drowning') he tells us how he became so much more personally efficient, effective and better able to focus on the essential stuff by journaling daily. He's since inspired a whole generation of worker bees to get scribing. So if the spiritual, creative side of writing fills you with horror, or indeed apathy, perhaps try looking at this practice through the lens of productivity at work, as a tool to cleanse your mind, refocus your attention and strategise better. Whichever approach you find most appealing, please give it a go, as this is low-effort, high-yield enrichment. As a pursuit leading to personal growth its potential is limitless.

FEED YOUR SOUL

'You will enrich your life immeasurably if you approach it with a sense of wonder and discovery, and always challenge yourself to try new things.'
– Nate Berkus

Capture the moments that matter to you in ways that enrich your soul, whether through canvas portrait photography or diary entries that bring to mind everything that happened that day, or through reflective meditation and stillness – whatever enlivens you and preserves your treasured moments. I was so impassioned by preserving memories I created a business out of helping others 'capture treasured memories in art and rhyme': it was a total joy to spread the magic of giving in this way for a decade, and I still feel truly blessed by my experience of creating and leading The Bespoke Gift Company. What is it that makes time stand still for you? When do you feel at your most lucid in the moment, and able to capture every sensation? How can you do more of that?

MAKE YOUR HOME A HAVEN

'Home is where the heart is.'
– Anon.

I find creative joy in tending to my home and garden, and I take pride in making every room a sensual delight for me and anyone who joins me. It doesn't have to be lavish interior design; I have renovated numerous homes now on super-tight budgets, but always with a polished finish that makes my heart sing. From my daughter's Flower Fairy bedroom, with all the pretty finishing touches that I gathered for it, to my Louis XVI-inspired boudoir with its white organza, French chateau furniture and baroque wallpaper, to my Palladian-style orangery, designed to feel as though it's floating in the middle of a park, surrounded by lawn and greenery, light bursting in from every angle, I love it.

My home is my haven and I feel a thrill every time I arrive there or sit in any room or part of the garden. I simply feel at peace; I feel totally at home. If we remind ourselves that we have one life, and it is not a rehearsal, then why on earth wouldn't we create the most personally pleasing living space we could? Does arriving home fill you with joy? Is your bedroom an oasis of calm? Is the kitchen the warm heart of the house, filled with laughter and good company? Is the house filled with the people you love best? Your home is truly where your heart is, so personalise it to bring you maximum joy.

*   *   *

Now we are at the end of the six steps of the Energy-SCAPE™ programme and the start of a flourishing new you. If you've worked through the exercises in each chapter, you will already have made tremendous progress and will find yourself in a new zone. If you've skipped ahead to absorb the knowledge first, now is the time to work back through all of the exercises in turn and see for yourself how the theory delivers results. If you want to take it to the next level, how about taking the 'Kickstarter Six-Week Challenge'? – More about this in the concluding section.

Conclusion

'If one advances confidently in the direction of his dreams, and endeavours to live the life which he has imagined, he will meet with a success unexpected in common hours.'
  – Henry David Thoreau

At a recent seminar I hosted for Amazon staff, a woman lingered at the end of my session to request a private conversation. We huddled out of earshot of the pulsing room and she nervously asked, 'How do you manage the guilt?' She meant the guilt of failing to honour a pledge, a new habit or a new resolve. How to combat the self-loathing that bubbles noxiously, grating against rational thought. How to dismiss 'falling off the wagon' as okay and acceptable. My response to this, to her and to you, is to stop the pursuit of perfection.

I don't offer you this book as a bible of specificity. I encourage you to reach for those stars and to indeed follow your dreams, but without extreme behaviour, and without mental anguish. 'Progress not perfection' is a motto to live by. When I have idled a weekend away with my family, not working out, not eating well and not completing the work tasks I'd set myself on Friday, and yes, drinking too much alcohol, I don't waste Monday berating myself. Instead, I reflect on what I gained, for instance, the quality time with my children, 'rest days' off from pummelling my body in the gym, the laughs I had, and I apply a perspective that gives me context. I herald the self-acceptance.

In *The Gifts of Imperfection,* Brené Brown teaches us that 'Healthy striving is self-focused: "How can I improve?" Perfectionism is other-focused: "What will they think?"' So take heed: being your best self is not a dictate. It's an invitation. It's an opportunity. It's a way to contextualise life as a gift to be enjoyed not endured. How you define what is best for you is entirely up to you; and how you apply it again, equally so.

Women are fast to self-criticise but our personal growth arrives when we become *aware* not chiding. In her book *Lean In,* Sheryl Sandberg beseeches women to grab hold of self-compassion, as 'it allows us to respond to our own errors with concern and understanding rather than criticism and shame'. We must not blame ourselves for failing when in fact failure is normal, expected and always a moment of growth. As Elizabeth Day, author of *How to Fail,* tells us boldly, 'failure is key to our liberation'.

I hope that reading this book, reflecting and adopting some of the practices described here has revealed to you how powerful and proactive *you* can be. You alone know best how to bring the approaches that resonate most deeply with you into your daily life, how to blend new habits with existing commitments, and which new ways of living will enable you to grow in vitality and see your personal impact deepen. Keep the book beside you to revisit and refresh your inspiration whenever you need it. Use it, along with your journal, to look back over the journey you've been on and to explore where you could go next. Looking back over the path we've taken in these pages, as I do below, I believe that the reader finishing this book will have evolved from the one who started reading it – and I hope be a more vibrant, intentional and conscious one at that, on a new, positive path.

Let's remind ourselves of how we got here.

Energy

You've now learned that you have the power to take back control, to live life in a continually energised state adapted to your individual needs. You now know about the component parts of the Productivity Balance System that contribute to achieving optimal energetic harmony in your life. You know how to adjust the various components to the point of equilibrium in honour of your bio-individuality. It's up to you to identify when and where you're energised and when depleted, and to remedy your routines accordingly.

Self-awareness

Doing deep inner work is not selfish. Ultimately, connecting inwardly to who you truly are and what inspires you most reveals your natural path forward; it becomes your guiding force and taps into your subconscious self. You can't contribute or live life as your fullest, most radiant self without self-awareness – beyond self-awareness come self-care, self-love and a more permanent sense of presence. Once you learn to protect and nurture yourself everything becomes possible. Once you explore your personal values and your belief system, and understand how they affect your behaviours, you will see how aligning your work and your life with them will generate fulfilment and happiness; you will see the power in making self-awareness the key to unlocking your best self.

Cleansing

There is so much truth in the wise words of the Latin poet Juvenal: 'A healthy mind in a healthy body.' Alas, too much of what we are exposed to these days threatens the health of our minds and bodies: adulterated foods, a deluge of digital distractions of dubious value, lack of exercise or too much exercise, increasingly pressurised workplaces, untenable to-do lists. It's all too easy to passively submit to these negative forces and acquiescently drift down the stream of life. But with consciousness comes the ability to defend that healthy mind and body as you refine your choices, and grow stronger every day through purging whatever doesn't serve you and embracing that which will feed you in every sense.

Action

Now that you know the theory, and understand yourself better, it's time to put everything into action. Making the actions you want to take into habits is a way of making things easier – after all, you probably don't think twice about cleaning your teeth before you go to bed. Understanding cues and rewards to make the habits stick is liberating. Equally, being clear about why you're making changes, and precisely how they support your goals, will spur you on. When you reframe perceptions of certain actions, you can turn a seeming chore into a pleasure. Critical here is illuminating your vision with crystal clarity, knowing your purpose, writing your mission statement and the journey you want to go on (not just the destination end point).

Play

There is a widely recognised consensus from luminaries past and present as to why play is so vital to every aspect of our lives. No one has expressed it better than healer and poet Vince Gowmon: 'Play isn't something separate from the daily grind of life. It is not something to finally to get to when work ends. Rather, play, like music, is a force that we feel in our bones and that whispers in our heart.' Whatever the context – our professional lives, our creativity, purpose, relationships, learning, personal wellbeing and connection to our communities – play unlocks that next level of fulfilment, success and joy. I invite you to respect its glorious role in unleashing your best self. Go forth and have fun!

Enrichment

We have acknowledged the need to redefine success, to move away from striving for temporary highs and stop chasing meaningless societally contrived ideologies of success, such as power and wealth. We have looked at how to find soul in the daily grind. There are countless ways to enrich your life, and I have shared those that I have found most compelling. Nobody would dispute that showing kindness brings pleasure both to you and to others. Likewise, listening, caring and learning are all elevating. The potential for enrichment is unlimited. As you increase your own self-awareness, personal ideas may stimulate you: music, perhaps, or volunteering in an area of interest to you. In this respect, the world really is your oyster.

THE KICKSTART SIX-WEEK CHALLENGE

> *'"Someday" is a disease that will take your dreams to the grave with you. If it's important to you and you want to do it "eventually," just do it now and correct course along the way.'*
> – Timothy Ferriss

If you would relish a formal support structure to launch you on your 'Flourish' path, why not join me on my Kickstart Six-week Challenge, which will give you a defined start point (your baseline) and end point (your clarified goals), while enabling you to evaluate your progress throughout? Through this cumulative process, based on the Energy-SCAPE™ model, you will be able to build up your practice, deepen your self-examination and maximise your impact. Following this plan step by step will see you pushing out beyond your personal comfort zone to achieve a happier, more energetically balanced you with every passing day. You'll also enjoy the benefit of access to me and an encouraging community of like-minded ambitious women seeking a new definition of personal success.

All the resources you need for the Kickstart Six-week Challenge are available on my website, www.biancabest .com, along with inspirational stories and tips to keep you motivated, inspired and entertained along the way.

> *'The difference between failure and success is perseverance.'*
> – Arianna Huffington

* * *

A LETTER FROM THE HEART

Dear Flourisher,

I am incredibly excited by the huge potential of living a life of joy and balance. I hope I've stirred you to seize the precious adventure that is life and make yours even more vibrant and fulfilling.

I would love to continue our relationship and now invite you to join me on my journey of empowering more women to learn how to step into their best selves and embrace a life of balance. Read my blog, join one of my workshops, invite me to speak in your organisation, sign up for the six-week challenge (see above), follow me on social media or let me coach you personally. Whichever tickles your fancy, I'd love to hear from you and learn how I can serve you best.

Warm and sincere wishes for your personal version of success, and thank you from the bottom of my heart for reading my words. I'm blessed to have had your attention throughout.

Bianca x

References

Albom, M (2004) *The Five People You Meet in Heaven.*
London: Time Warner

Baldwin, C (1995) *Life's Companion.* New York:
Bantam Doubleday Dell Publishing Group

Bezos, J (1997) Amazon public shareholder letter,
1997, http://media.corporate-ir.net/media_files/irol/97
/97664/reports/Shareholderletter97.pdf

Brainyquote.com (n.d.) 'Deepak Chopra Quotes',
www.brainyquote.com/authors/deepak_chopra

Brand, R (2017) *Recovery: Freedom from Our Addictions.*
London: Bluebird, Pan Macmillan

Brown, B (2010) *The Gifts of Imperfection: Let Go of
Who You Think You're Supposed to Be and Embrace Who
You Are.* Center City, MN: Hazelden

Byrne, R (2006) *The Secret*. London: Simon & Schuster Ltd

Campbell-McBride, N (2018) *Gut and Psychology Syndrome: Natural Treatment for Autism, Dyspraxia, A.D.D., Dyslexia, A.D.H.D., Depression, Schizophrenia*, London: Medinform Publishing

Choquette, S (2004) *Trust Your Vibes*. London: Hay House Inc.

Coelho, P (2012) *The Alchemist: A Fable About Following Your Dream*. London: Harper Collins Publishers

Covey, S (1989) *Seven Habits of Highly Effective People*. London: Simon & Schuster Ltd

Crane, K (2017) '8 Ways Meditation Can Improve Your Life', *Huffington Post*, www.huffpost.com/entry/meditation-benefits_n_5842870

Day, E (2019) *How to Fail: Everything I've Ever Learned from Things Going Wrong*. London: Harper Collins Publishers

Dooley, M (2017) *Playing the Matrix: A Program for Living Deliberately*. London: Hay House

Duffy, W (2002) *Sugar Blues*, New York: Warner Books

Duhigg, C (2012) *The Power of Habit*. London: Random House

Ferriss, T (2007) *The 4-Hour Workweek*. New York: Crown Publishing

Frankl, V (2004) *Man's Search for Meaning*. New York: Random House

Friedman, T (2017) *Thank You For Being Late: An Optimist's Guide to Thriving in the Age of Accelerations*. New York: Penguin

Gameau, D (dir.) (2015) *That Sugar Film*

Gerber, M E (2001)*The E-Myth Revisited: Why Most Small Businesses Don't Work and What to Do About It*. New York: HarperCollins Publishers

Goleman, G (2013) *Focus: The Hidden Driver of Excellence*. New York: Harper Collins Publisher

goodreads.com (n.d.) 'Howard Thurman Quotes', www.goodreads.com/quotes/8676665-it-s-a-wondrous-thing-that-a-decision-to-act-releases

Gowman, V (n.d.) 'Playful Quotes for the Child in Your Heart', http://newearthmarketing.com/vincegowmons/playful-quotes-for-the-child-in-your-heart

Groth, L (2019) 'How Sobriety Changed Bradley Cooper's Life and Made "A Star Is Born" Possible', www.livestrong.com/article/13717378-bradley-cooper -addiction-sobriety-sober

Hamilton, D (2010) *Why Kindness Is Good for You*. London: Hay House

Hicks, E and Hicks, J (2004) *Ask and It Is Given: Learning to Manifest You Desires (the Law of Attraction)*. Carlsbad, CA: Hay House

Kimsey-House, H, Kimsey-House, K, Whitworth, L and Sandahl, P (2009) Co-active Coaching: Changing Businesses Transforming Lives. Boston, MA: Nicholas Brealey Publishing

Kipp, M (2017) *Claim Your Power: A 40-day Journey to Dissolve the Hidden Blocks that Keep You Stuck and Finally Thrive in Your Life's Unique Purpose.* Carlsbad, CA: Hay House Inc.

LaPorte, D (2014) *The Desire Map: A Guide to Creating Goals with Soul*, Canada: Danielle La Porte Inc.

Malchiodi, C (2014) 'Creative Arts Therapy and Expressive Arts Therapy', https://www .psychologytoday.com/gb/blog/arts-and-health /201406/creative-arts-therapy-and-expressive-arts -therapy

McKeown, G (2014) *Essentialism: The Disciplined Pursuit of Less*. New York: Crown Publishing

Morrissey, H (2018) *A Good Time to Be a Girl*. Glasgow: William Collins

Perlmutter, D (2014) *Grain Brain: The Surprising Truth about Wheat, Carbs, and Sugar – Your Brain's Silent Killers*. London: Yellow Kite Books

Robbins, A (1989) *Unlimited Power*. London: Simon & Schuster Ltd

Sandberg, S (2015) *Lean In: Women, Work, and the Will to Lead*. New York: Penguin Random House

Shakespeare, W (2001) *Twelfth Night*. London: Wordsworth Editions Limited

Shapiro, S (2017) *The Power of Mindfulness: What you practice grows stronger* (TED Talk), www.youtube.com /watch?v=IeblJdB2-Vo

Sinek, S (2009) *Start with Why*. New York: Penguin Group

Singer, M A (2007) *The Untethered Soul: The Journey Beyond Yourself*. Oakland, CA: New Harbinger Publishing

Stillman, J (2019) 'Here Are the Personal Mission Statements of Musk, Branson, and Oprah (Plus 7

Questions to Write Your Own)', www.inc.com/jessica
-stillman/how-to-write-your-own-personal-mission
-statement-7-questions.html

The Guardian (2014) 'Maya Angelou Quotes: 15 of the
Best', www.theguardian.com/books/2014/may/28
/maya-angelou-in-fifteen-quotes

The Leaders Brain (no date) 'CEO of the Brain',
www.theleadersbrain.org/overview/ceo.html

Thoreau, H D (1854) *Walden: Or, Life in the Woods*

Tolle, E (1999) *The Power of Now*. Novato, CA: New
World Library

Tribole, E (2012) *Intuitive Eating: A Revolutionary
Program that Works*. New York: St Martin's Press

Vozza, S (2014) 'Personal Mission Statements of 5
Famous CEOs (and Why You Should Write One
Too)', www.fastcompany.com/3026791/personal
-mission-statements-of-5-famous-ceos-and-why-you
-should-write-one-too

Wallace, J (2017) 'Why It's Good for Grown-ups to
Go Play', www.washingtonpost.com/national/health
-science/why-its-good-for-grown-ups-to-go-play/2017
/05/19/99810292-fd1f-11e6-8ebe-6e0dbe4f2bca_story
.html?noredirect=on&utm_term=.e06f90b10435

Ward, N (2017) 'Marginal Gains: It's Not About the Bike', www.thedrum.com/opinion/2017/08/04/marginal-gains-its-not-about-the-bike

Williamson, M (1992) *A Return to Love.* New York: HarperCollins

Wilson, S (2014) *I Quit Sugar: Your Complete 8-Week Detox Program and Cookbook.* London: Macmillan Publishers

Winfrey, O (2013) 'Caroline Myss' Advice for Getting to the Heart of Who You Really Are' (Interview), www.oprah.com/spirit/caroline-myss-interview-with-oprah-winfrey

Acknowledgements

Thank you to my family for letting me escape to beaches, woodlands, hilltops, cafes, hotels and my favourite spot, bed (!) to write this book. I appreciate every moment of respectful solitude as a gift. You've enabled me to flourish and I'm forever grateful.

Thank you to my editor, Verity Ridgman, for tirelessly culling my effusive words.

Thank you to the team at Rethink Press for pushing me to hit my deadlines.

And finally, thank you to MediaCom for supporting my adventures.

Appendix: Values Inspiration

Accountability
Accuracy
Achievement
Adventurousness
Altruism
Ambition
Assertiveness
Balance
Belonging
Boldness
Calmness
Carefulness
Challenge
Cheerfulness
Commitment
Community
Compassion
Competitiveness
Consistency
Contentment

Contribution
Control
Cooperation
Correctness
Courtesy
Creativity
Curiosity
Decisiveness
Dependability
Determination
Devoutness
Diligence
Discipline
Discretion
Diversity
Dynamism
Economy
Effectiveness
Efficiency
Elegance

Empathy
Enjoyment
Enthusiasm
Equality
Excellence
Excitement
Expertise
Exploration
Expressiveness
Fairness
Faith
Fidelity
Fitness
Fluency
Focus
Freedom
Fun
Generosity
Goodness
Grace
Growth
Happiness
Hard Work
Health
Helping Society
Holiness
Honesty
Honour
Humility
Independence
Ingenuity
Inner Harmony

Inquisitiveness
Insightfulness
Intelligence
Intellectual Status
Intuition
Joy
Justice
Leadership
Legacy
Love
Loyalty
Making a difference
Mastery
Merit
Obedience
Openness
Order
Originality
Patriotism
Perfection
Piety
Positivity
Practicality
Preparedness
Professionalism
Prudence
Quality Orientation
Reliability
Resourcefulness
Restraint
Security
Self-actualisation

Self-control
Selflessness
Self-reliance
Sensitivity
Serenity
Service
Shrewdness
Simplicity
Soundness
Speed
Spontaneity
Stability
Strategic
Strength
Structure
Success

Support
Teamwork
Temperance
Thankfulness
Thoroughness
Thoughtfulness
Timeliness
Tolerance
Traditionalism
Trustworthiness
Truth-seeking
Understanding
Uniqueness
Usefulness
Vision
Vitality

The Author

B ianca Best is an award-winning advertising agency executive, entrepreneur, mother of four – and a living example of balance. She began her career in journalism and moved into advertising before starting her own technology busi-ness, which she ran from home while looking after her young children. After an exhilarating decade of entrepreneurialism, more recently she has embraced a global leadership role in the world's largest media agency, running an emerging technology division. Bianca continues to describe her CV as a chronology of passions explored and has a personal mission to create business cultures that are rich in authenticity, productivity and kindness.

A certified leadership coach, hypnotherapist and neuro-linguistic practitioner, Bianca is dedicated to inspiring and motivating ambitious individuals to maximise their impact. She teaches that with conscious and intentional living, balance and joy are achievable. She empowers women to flourish as their best selves by hosting wellbeing events, both privately and for large corporates such as Amazon; through keynotes at global conferences such as Women in Silicon Valley; through individual coaching; and by offering inspiring insight and effective leadership advice at www.biancabest.com, and female-oriented life hacks on her own woman-to-woman skill share site, www.yourlifehack.com.

Contact

✉ bianca@biancabest.com
🔗 www.linkedin.com/in/biancabest
⦿ www.instagram.com/biancabest_
🐦 www.twitter.com/BiancaBest1
📘 www.facebook.com/yourlifehackers
🌐 www.biancabest.com
🌐 www.yourlifehack.com

Lightning Source UK Ltd.
Milton Keynes UK
UKHW020619050619
343910UK00006B/190/P